The Forward Book of Poetry

2024

T0322530

The Forward Book of Poetry

2024

Forward
Prizes
for Poetry

First published in Great Britain by
Forward Arts Foundation · Somerset House Exchange
The Strand · London · WC2R 1LA
in association with
Faber & Faber Ltd · The Bindery · 51 Hatton Garden · London EC1N 8HN

ISBN 978 0 571 38334 4 (paperback)

Typeset by Hamish Ironside

Printed and bound by CPI Group (UK) · Croydon CRO 4YY

A CIP catalogue reference for this book
is available at the British Library

To Giles Spackman

Contents

The Forward Prize for Best Single Poem – Written Shortlisted poems

Highly Commended Poems

Preface

Voice is at the heart of poetry. It's the holy grail for emerging poets: any number of writing workshops focus on a writer '*finding*' this quality, and, as readers, it's one of the first things we notice: the turns of phrase unique to a writer, their syntax and language, the cadence of their words as they spill from a pen.

I'm sitting in front of my window, and as the voices of my neighbours float up from the garden, it occurs how fitting this use of voice is. That toddler's delighted squeals sound like no other, and the neighbour warbling along to the radio is immediately more whole. Voice is central to the human experience, whether on the page or open air. (There's also the buzz of an electric saw, which adds some urgency to these proceedings.)

These 2023 prizes open a new chapter for Forward, as we launch our first-ever performance category, giving poets' voices another dimension. To our minds, this isn't a new initiative: it's long overdue. We want to address some of the historical inequities in the way our broad church has viewed its congregation. Performance has been the lifeblood of our art form from the start. Poetry began as an oral tradition: verse was composed to be performed and passed from generation to generation, carried on that precious voice. And yet, performance is often left out of prestigious awards like ours.

Its inclusion now feels very much in keeping with the vision at the heart of our work: Forward aims to showcase the best new poetry and to build bigger, more diverse audiences for poetry. Our aim is to focus on the *new*, the *contemporary*, and to use poetry to capture the lived experience of the world today.

This fourth category increases the ways poets can access the Forward Prizes. It's the first open to submissions from the poets themselves, as well as producers. It gives poets another arena in which to shine, as many already move fluidly between the written and performed forms.

The category also allows audiences more ways to engage with poetry, as we now have a digital companion to this annual Forward Book of Poetry: on page 9 you'll find a QR code that will enable you to view all the videos shortlisted and highly commended for the performance prize this year.

This was a huge undertaking and involved two judging panels this year, one chaired by Joelle Taylor that focused solely on the two single poem categories, comprising poets who excelled both on the page and on the stage, as well as a collections panel chaired by Bernardine Evaristo.

We extend our immense gratitude to all the partners, producers and poets who advised us through this process. It was a challenge, and we have lots of ideas on how to improve for next year. The judges on the single poems panel heroically debated the rationale behind the new prize and kept our mission and vision at the heart of their discussions, while also challenging and holding us to account.

This year's judges read 236 full collections and read and watched 420 single poems. To arrive at a shortlist of five in each category was a daunting task for our esteemed judges. Discussions volleyed between the merits of the individual texts to much larger, theoretical discussions about what prizes are for, and how we can assess the merit of a writer's larger project: is it better to aim boldly and fail, or to play it safe and be word perfect? One of the judges framed their task as an act of curation, recognising that a list compiled in this year would be different from a list compiled in any other, as the works speak not just to each other, but to the particular time we're living in now. We hope their assembly here will be considered in this spirit.

None of the prizes, of course, would be possible without the dedication of our ten judges this year: the Best Collections panel chaired by Booker Prize winner Bernardine Evaristo, including poets Kate Fox, Karen McCarthy Woolf, Andrés N Ordorica and Jessica Traynor; and the Best Single Poems panel, chaired by TS Eliot Prize winner Joelle Taylor, with poets Caroline Bird, Khadijah Ibrahiim, Chris Redmond and Sue Roberts.

We are grateful to our funders: Bookmark Content, which has supported us from the very beginning; Arts Council England; the Charlotte Aitken Trust; John Ellerman Foundation; the Felix Dennis Estate, which generously supports the Best First Collection Prize; Garfield Weston Foundation; Harold Hyam Wingate Foundation and a number of individual donors.

Thank you, too, to fellow Trustees of the Forward Arts Foundation: Jamie Andrews, Mary Amanuel, Kim Evans, Aoife O'Connor, Maya Ophelia, Latinka Pilipovic and Amelia Richards.

Thank you as always to the Forward Arts Foundation team, which continues to chart new territories even as they navigate challenges in an era of unprecedented change.

And, finally, a note to you, dear reader: if you've picked up this book and found joy in its pages, I encourage you to share it with friends and family. Consider giving it as a gift this Christmas or for a birthday. Many of us discovered a much-beloved poem after it was shared by someone we love. As a small charity, your investment in this book is vital to our survival.

William Sieghart
Founder of the Forward Prizes for Poetry
June 2023

The Forward Book of Poetry
2024

Introduction

Reading so many collections of poetry for the Forward Prizes was an intensely rewarding experience, one where I was able luxuriate in the music of language and tune my ear and sensibilities to the preoccupations and aesthetics of today's poets. With over 230 books submitted, the reading also felt educational; here was a large cross-section of newly minted poetry books published in English, ranging from debut authors to their more seasoned counterparts. Devouring so many collections within a compacted period of time, I found myself engaging with the subjectivities, intellectual interrogations, narrative threads, private interiorities, frailties and emotional sensitivities of contemporary poetry. While individuality is inherent in the form, and is indeed a prerequisite – surely we want poetry to offer us something unique – there was nonetheless a sense of tapping into the collective unconscious, a sense of a 21st-century zeitgeist that feels quite distinct from the preceding century, even though that ended a mere two decades or so ago.

Our poetry publishing has changed and expanded to include people from a wider range of communities. It's heartening for someone such as myself, who has long campaigned to see this happen, and it is regenerative for the sector – new voices, fresh perspectives, expanded audiences and readerships.

The jury for the Forward's two collection prizes consisted of myself as Chair, along with the poets Kate Fox, Karen McCarthy Woolf, Andrés N Ordorica and Jessica Traynor. Our discussions were lively, educated, generous and honest. For our shortlists, we were drawn to poets who felt as if they could only have been writing now – even if they're not writing about this present time. We wanted to select poetry that didn't feel as if it could have been written 10 or 20 years ago – in either form, or subject matter, or ideally both.

Like other art forms, such as theatre, dance, film and the visual arts, poetry needs to progress, to push against expectations, to move from its established foundations to new modes of expression, to reinvent itself as it responds to the changing times. If it does not, it risks stagnation, the fossilisation of the imagination, rather than feeling dynamic and alive.

We were also drawn to poets who engage with both the self and society, even when their writing is at its most lyric, its most intensely personal. It goes without saying that the outcome of a literary prize is determined by its jury, which for most awards changes every year, and rightly so. A different jury might well have made different choices. I'm interested in the ways in which the media sometimes reduces poetry to simplistic tropes that fit into its politics, creating the impression of proselytization; poetry without nuance and complexity. Poets of colour are sometimes described as writing about identity, or migration, or racism, when they are often clearly not – full stop; and when they are, this is never all they are doing. It is lazy critical analysis and often overlooks sophisticated thematic explorations. That said, poetry is always 'about' something – depending on the gaze, the interpretation, and all poetry can be viewed through a political context – small c. Poetry is always about more than just 'language' because you cannot extract language from culture, context, community. Poetry does not float in a universe of nothingness.

As an art form, poetry needs movement and metamorphosis. Perhaps the greatest movement in poetry of recent times is the launch of the AI chatbot, ChatGPT, on 30 November 2022. ChatGPT is a software predator with the capability to create original poetry from scouring everything on the internet, which it ingests into its mammoth brain ready for our questions and instructions; these might be to write a poem, a novel, an essay. Other chatbots are proliferating that offer the same instant creative-writing facilities. You can imagine the potential, and you can imagine the problems, all of which are being documented in the media as I write this.

Suddenly we are in a climate where poetry as we know it might be on the decline. I've asked ChatGPT to write several poems thus far, and while they've been clichéd and pretty terrible – as is some poetry written by humans, if we're honest – it will move beyond that in the future as the chatbots become ever more sophisticated. Already we have a distinction that didn't exist last year: poetry written by humans and poetry written by chatbots.

I know what I prefer. This poetry anthology, written by humans, one hopes, reads beautifully, with moments of daring experimentation, cultural engagement and the profound reflection that connects us to our deeper, often unsayable feelings. When a formidable AI foe emerges and poses a potential existential threat to our literature and creativity, it should serve to remind us that, irrespective of our preferences and differences, poetry written by humans is to be cherished and protected; and we must be prepared to fight for its survival.

Bernardine Evaristo
Chair of the judges for the Forward Prize for Best Collection
and the Felix Dennis Prize for Best First Collection
June 2023

Introduction

It was only recently, after a lifetime of studying and engineering poetry, that I remembered something I knew as a child but had forgotten. Poetry is not the answer. It is the question. That fundamental truth is mirrored in the works included within this anthology, a collection of contemporary British and Irish poetry at its most curious and alive. This book reflects an exciting time for the UK and Ireland in poems that are unflinching, dissident and defiant. It is a restless poetic, a poetry of urgency that is expressed for the first time in a major British literary prize in both its written and performed forms. A 21st-century poetry prize should seek to reflect the diversity in form and subject that is at the heart of the art. This is the beginning of a process to include performed poetry, which exists primarily in its live iteration, a poetic that is distinct and valuable, a poetry of breath, of belief and connection. It is an embodied poetic that queries the margins. The live poet negotiates with air as forensically as the published poet reckons with white space. Consequently, the margins have never been so close to the centre of the page.

As a panel, we were gifted with a stunning array of written and performed works that led to the vibrant conversations and beautiful disagreements that are at the core of democracy. As a panel, we were as passionate and exploratory in our thinking as the works submitted to us. It was a thrilling process.

I have written elsewhere that the writing of a poem is an act of resistance and the performance of it, a revolution. It is gratifying that now some of the more impressive works in live poetry (or spoken word) operate as meaningfully on the page as they do in the spotlight. This was clear to us as a panel. There is a new understanding that it is possible for us as writers to use all the mechanisms at our disposal and to eschew the constant faux battle between what is written and what is spoken. I call it 'faux' because it feels like a construct, a deliberate division. Once, there were only words and different ways of using them. The quest to separate the pen from the mouth is perhaps class-based, a taxonomy of poetry that places the academic and obscure at the top of a precarious pile of books which has spoken word as its foundation.

I am thrilled that the Forward Prizes for Poetry are addressing these commonalities and differences in approach; I hope that it will lead to not just the idea of form being expanded, but the potential narratives too. We need poetry that is *of* us, that is *because of* us and not just *for* us.

Joelle Taylor
Chair of the judges for the Forward Prizes for
Best Single Poem – Written and Performed
June 2023

The Forward Prize for Best Single Poem –
Performed
Shortlisted poems

Zena Edwards
Human: This Embodied Knowledge

Nidhi Zak/Aria Eipe
And our eyes are on Europe

Michael Pedersen
The Cat Prince

Bohdan Piasecki
Almost Certainly

Roger Robinson
The City Kids See the Sea

The Forward Prize for Best Collection
Selected poems from the shortlisted books

Jason Allen-Paisant

The Picture and the Frame

1.

I have found no word for the effect of the light on the water
other than *mare=ballerina*, the one Gino Severini invented.

*

Nothing makes sense until it makes sense in the body, till the
body is present at the making-sense.

*

There's a set of people selling small things on the Piazza San
Marco. What should we call these small things, since what
they actually are doesn't matter? They throw these things in
the air. I approach one, asking what they are. *Lanza*, he says.
A toy for kids. For demonstration, he throws one, catching
it back. *8 euros*, he says. There's this set of people. I've seen
them seeing with their feet, their backs, their entire bodies.
I've seen them knowing when to run from the police before
the police are in sight. Have you seen them too?

*

Eight years I've been trying to name this recognition
expressed in my flesh.

*

Mare=Ballerina is supposedly about a dancer, one who, in her
movement, evokes the crashing of the waves on the seashore.
For me, it evoked the light over the Canal and its houses,
the Venice I saw, wondering what The Moor saw, that Moor
who arrived here at such a point in the 16th century that he

could have been at home in Carpaccio's *Miracle of the Relic of the Cross at the Rialto Bridge*. That he could have been *that* gondolier, the sharp looking dude. That Venice, that canal, that light seen from the oriental windows.

*

The Venice expressed in my flesh, as if the spirit of the sea of back home was also here.

*

Where you from? The people selling the small things greet me like this when my eyes meet theirs. It's the only way to greet, as if to say, *why, who, you, here – you who see me.*

Ali, 21, from Senegal guesses at where I'm from in Africa. He sells bracelets.

Buy a bracelet to support me, pour me soutenir. We bond through the French language. We move around in the wide world, forced into fluidity. It's not my style but, of course. He gives me an additional one for free. *Porte-bonheur. Pour les enfants.*

2.

In Veronese's *Feast at the Home of Levi*, conceived in fact as a depiction of *The Last Supper* before the artist's brush with the Inquisition, a young, dark-skinned man dressed in red tunic and turban shares the frame with Jesus and the apostles.

All of a sudden, with Veronese's hedonistic canvas, one enters a time without really entering it. The painting becomes a joke on the viewer. A door to a chamber is shown without any key whatsoever to access it. One's only consolation is to say,

I have seen that we were here, so normally here, in another time.

Without any witness (writing, inscriptions, books, legends) tying that time to the present, all the stories have to be invented— reinvented.

*

In the window of Nardi, the jeweller's, there are Blackamoor brooches. There are rings made of diamonds and rubies with miniature heads of turbaned Moors in sculpted ebony.

*

The intervening history of the representation of my body in text.

*

For Veronese, this painting was all about invention, and for it, he took huge license with theological doctrine.

*

There are Moor heads everywhere. We're not talking about this.

*

One wonders what kind of a character he is, this red-turbaned African man present at the banquet of a Renaissance prince. He's talking to a fat white man dressed in fancier robes. The fat dude looks into the distance distractedly. One can't help but notice the wily look on African dude's face, but only after a while do you notice his hand reaching into the other man's bag. Disappointing to say the least. The other African figures in the canvas occupy subservient roles, like pages, but they're also comfortably there. They're looking people in the eye, even having conversation. Ambiguous. But with ambiguity, I find myself stepping into a different history of representation. Ambiguity is a fucking revolution. It's almost overwhelming.

*

All I have is invention. All I could ever do is invent. I was tired of invention.

*

There's all the stuff that the European viewer can't see, all the stuff they haven't allowed themselves to see.

*

The Moor remains invisible, despite the obsession with his body.

Self-Portrait as Othello II

The Black body is signed as physically and psychically open space ... A space not simply owned by those who embody it but constructed and occupied by other embodiments. Inhabiting it is a domestic, hemispheric ... transatlantic ... international pastime. There is a playing around in it.
                    Dionne Brand, *A Map to the Door of No Return*

You left home for a wandering lust for pain
    had driven you to the edge of yourself & wanting
to open the windows of life you decided to migrate to this
    country. You came for a different sound

the quaintness of gestures of faces & food. New tongues
    are something like trophies *faccia* faces *façades* ...
The façade hides things you like this each new word
    an erotic death your language grows with buried things.

What does it mean to be *far more fair than black?*
    Education speech dress learning. You have the brawn
of an intellectual rude boy sturdier in brain-work
    than in war. Know streets and livity talk Shakespeare

Baudelaire Dante and Nietzsche talk sound system. What actually
    is the language of where you're from? It's that familiarity
with rough life that eye of struggle that smell of fight
    hardness of speech a coming up vibe Oxford and all

that she likes so invites you to visit at Christmas three whole days
    with family and one party to the next but they think
it's going to pass this fascination with the dark-skinned boy surely
    she'll come around find someone of her kind   *when she is sated.*

Alvise Da Cada Mosto, a Venetian, in the service of Don Henry of Portugal, informs us in his preface, that he was the first navigator from the noble city of Venice who had sailed on the ocean beyond the Straits of Gibraltar, to the southern parts of Negroland, and Lower Ethiopia. These voyages are the oldest extant and were first printed at Venice in 1507.

He considered the rivers Senegal and Rio Grande to be branches of the Niger, by which means the Europeans might open a trade with the rich kingdoms of Tombuto and Melli on that river, and thus bring gold from the countries of the Negroes, by an easier, safer, and more expeditious manner, than as conveyed by the Moors of Barbary by land, over the vast and dangerous deserts that intervene between the country on the Niger and Senegal rivers, and Barbary. As, by the account of Leo, salt is the most valuable commodity throughout the countries of the Negroes, Ramusio proposed that the ships should take in cargoes of salt at the island of Sal and thence supply the countries on the Niger, which was reported to be navigable for 500 miles into the interior; and that they should bring back gold and slaves in return; the latter to be brought to market at St Jago, another of the Cape de Verd islands, where they would be immediately bought up for the West Indies.

Mary Jean Chan

Love for the Living

What does it mean to want to live? Only this:
to refuse to see the mouth's anguish as a sign

to step out of an open window. To refuse to be
thirty and afraid of leaving one city for another.

To refuse to be a bomb shelter for your mother's
fears. What is it like to believe the years are not

a life sentence for bodies like yours? Like this:
a spiral of rainbow bunting sprung like relief

across a lit sky. The ache when your father
mentions your partner's name. How you'd

notice, incredulous, the way no one cares as
you stand in the open, holding her, kissing.

from **Ars Poetica**

XIII

As a child, I often considered the impact that falling
in love with English had on my mother's happiness.
She once said, don't think you can talk back to me in
a colonial language, it isn't superior! I can't describe

her voice – when she speaks in Shanghainese – it is
sweet like water. Her language came to me as in a
familiar dream, a lotus flower sinking into my self
and blooming. During my first month in England,

I learnt the art and science of speaking to reassure.
How else can I survive? It's so easy to be ashamed.
I am asked why my poems are so clear. I'll confess:
it's what happens when you want to be understood.

Ten years ago, I found myself in Nice and learnt to
dream in French, my mother's first foreign tongue.
That summer, the sea was also my mother, the Bay
of Angels held me in its polyphony, and I chose all

my loves – Cantonese, English, Mandarin, French –
spoke with a satisfaction I had not felt in years, saw
my relationship to the world through sounds again,
till I was reconciled, the way rainbows exist in rain.

Jane Clarke

Spalls

To help us grow a garden, my mother and father travelled
across the Bog of Allen and over the Wicklow Gap.

They'd have preferred to drive west to Galway or Mayo,
they'd have preferred a husband and children

but their daughter loved a woman. We'd have the table set
for breakfast: rashers, black pudding, fried bread and eggs.

When the soil had warmed, we unloaded shovels
and rakes, buckets of compost and the rusted iron bar

for prising out rocks. The back seat was thronged
with pots of seedlings my mother had nurtured all winter.

We worked to her bidding: *loosen tangled roots before planting,
sow marigolds next to beans, sprinkle Epsom salts around roses.*

My father took off on his own to spud ragwort or clip a hedge.
One day he spent hours gathering stones of different shapes and
    sizes.

By evening he'd built us a wall under the holly, held together
by gravity and friction, hearted with handfuls of spalls.

At Purteen Harbour

Basking sharks, docile as seal pups,
harpooned and netted from currachs,

were towed one by one to the fishery
at the slipway. Fathers and sons

sliced off dorsal fins and hacked
through blubber to reach oil-filled livers.

Sweating in burn house heat,
they shovelled bleeding flesh

into the rendering machine.
They couldn't wash the smell

from their skin, not if they swam
to Inis Gealbhan at the end of every shift.

Year by year the catch diminished,
disappeared.

But late last April, old men
cheered from the headland, and said

It's as if we've been forgiven –
a school of twelve cruised into Keem Bay,

moon tails swishing, fins proud
as yawl sails above the waves.

Kit Fan

Mother's Ink

somewhere in the pre-history of ink is reproduction
                                    – Caitríona O'Reilly

Born I was, and wasn't.
She drew breath from the breath she'd lost
to phantom explosions inside her.
Three days, three nights, all breaths
and no food or sleep.

What other mothers had done she did,
re-staging the contractions until my departure.
I saw what she saw:
a cloud of messy flesh waiting at the gate
redder than ink.

The hard plastic on the suction cap.
My misshapen head.
What she remembered I remembered.
A cloudless day at 3 p.m.
and no ink was spilled as she kept herself to herself.

Now and then words escaped from her
bleached hands.
She knew I wanted ink greedily.
She fed it to me, dark milk diluted with water
that, when it touched a page, spread.

She knew it came from the clouds
hiding the teargas and bullets.
She only wanted good ink for me but feared what it meant.
I wanted just ink for her.
I wanted ink more than her.

Delphi

IF
time is heat
travelling
from hot
to cold
when is
the hour
date
location
of my death
?
Would I be
accompanied
?
Someone
holding
my hand
putting a
bitter mint in
my mouth
?
Would
morphine be
administered
?
How cold
could my
toes get
before they
fall off
?
Would there
be a setting
sun
?

IF
my severed
head
were to be
frozen
could I still
retrieve
a memory
file
from 24th
August 2017
the swim I
had
with Hugh
by the
harbour in
Trani and the
Michelin-
starred
dinner that
followed
?
Would it be
possible to
relish
the
handmade
tagliatelle
with
langoustines
again
?
Or the risotto
nero
?
How much
would the
access
cost
?

IF
I were to be
cast away
in the river
of blood
in the
Seventh
Circle with
the citizens
of Sodom
and
Gomorrah
would my
husband
be there
?
What
equipment
if any could
withstand
the barren
plain
of sand
ignited by the
flakes
of fire
?
Would
the guards
take bribes
?
Would the
fact that we
were both
decent
swimmers
help
?

IF
against the
odds I were
reincarnated
as a Japanese
maple
Higasayama
what would
stop me
from being
turned into
a bonsai tree
?
And IF
I cohabited
well with
the aphids
and bull-
finches
would I be
personified
in the next
cycle
?
What sins
should I
accumulate
to avoid
being human
again
?

IF
in the end
there is
nothingness
not even
the ink
and the
clouds would
nothing then
be left
of me
?
What would
happen
to the books
I read
and the
books
I wrote
?
Would
the memory
of the pages
I loved and
the memory
of my pages
loved by
others
fade away
equally
in the light-
years of
reading
?

IF
what you told
Oribasius
is true and
the speaking
water
has been
silenced
why are the
seas rising
?
Why do we
have more
kings
with splendid
halls
sprouting
high from
the ground
?
And IF
Phoebus
has lost
his house and
the laurel's
tongue
is cut
why am I
here
?
What are
the words
that can
never be
silenced
?

Elisabeth Sennitt Clough

bormed

they stick to me, those wonky-handled years –
nights of chip fat and dripping, a briny stench
of boiling bacon from a two-ring stove,
my blazer pocket damp with sly handfuls
of *you'll sit there 'til you eat it* boiled cabbage.
mum's tongue moving over consonants
in ways us hayseeds never learned, my brothers
insult each other, sail their yellow boat
through cloudy bathwater, take turns
to skipper a safe passage between jetties
of blue band margarine tubs. the water is cold,
time slow. in the front room, mum's wallpaper
wears nicotine stains and patches of damp
on the fleur-de-lys repeat. the decorator's signature,
barry 1986, hides behind the clock in cursive pencil.
this is the world young widowhood created,
codeine bottles and cotton balls beneath her bed,
a nightstand cluttered with bottles of empty scent,
pillows splashed with gin from those times she didn't
steady me for the razor blades and condoms, the guck
and brawn of stepdaddies and uncle-daddies:
come you here, fratchy gow, come you here, their prints
in castrol gtx over the back-kitchen door –
it's been four decades and i'm still bormed
by those years, whining at inattentive gods
to just let a good rain rumble and pour.

abecedarian for the vagina

after him, i just want to own myself again
but some days i imagine his residue
casually lolling about inside me
daubed on my cervix like ghost slime
every vagina he touched is probably googling its future self –
fanny fix, genital aesthetic surgery, labiaplasty, cosmetic gynaecology
gucci cucci. my friend kim laughs
how i'd have to save for eighteen months just to be scraped
i should ask him to pay for it
just a little re-texturising
kim says her ex told her she was *too fleshy*
like skate wings – as if
male genitals should be large and prominent and female genitals as lack
no one wants chopped liver between her legs, he told her, *you need to*
offer it up smooth
oyster on the half-shell, kim and i call our cunts posh names
pudendum, she says, *that high falutin' word comes from the latin for*
shame
quim, i say, my gran said it with such gusto she made it sound like a
restorative drink
reject all who tell you the new vag is just the same old pussy having shed
its winter coat
sphynx vs angora because all men want in life is a bald kitty
tautness is the hymen re-attached option with botox as an additional
extra, a brochure reads
upstream from the beaver family then, i say
victoria, kim gives her imaginary new vag a name
when i'm out with victoria, i'll feel like the queen of sheba
xerical references are not ideal, we laugh
you ever wonder what'd happen if we stopped looking at
ourselves through a man's mirror? kim asks
zero men, their mirrors, their cum shifting inside us like plankton

The Felix Dennis Prize for Best First Collection
Selected poems from the shortlisted books

Susannah Dickey

* Outtake #3

To be a woman and interested (in an anthropologically
detached way) in another woman's murder isn't subversive
anymore. It's as brave as eating
battery farmed chicken or setting fire to a crash test dummy.
If a thing's very purpose is suffering it isn't radical
to enjoy inflicting violence upon it.
But wait – the study of canonical violence
isn't the same as the infliction of violence.
But looking at an act isn't the same as studying it.
And witnessing an act isn't the same as committing it.
So, I guess we're at an impasse.
Somewhere between depravity and righteousness.
And where's that?
The recent market demand for velodromes,
I suppose. We can edit this later. Throw in some xylophones.

* Sex sells

Today the podcast hosts are speculating about Isdal's lovers.
We're picturing them lining up to varnish her antiques over

a long weekend, he says. They're saying, Hey, whatcha thinking?
as they brush her hair behind her ear (belt buckles clinking).

They're maligning her weird accent and her poor elocution
but still wanting her. A woman couldn't stay in one location

for so long without having anyone, the hosts say. She's not an art
installation or a cold front. She'd depart

if she had no one – go elsewhere. They're inclined
to think there was a man. He must have lured her up the incline.

Did you know that 50%
of murdered women are murdered, a docent

tells them, by their partners, or ex-partners?
(The prospect of a woman dying single is a greater disheartener

than this fact, though.) When a woman is killed the police
should talk to the lovers, he says. Look, she says, look at the ice

-made divots. There are inlets from the sea formed by glaciers.
The amorous looks Isdal must have got, he says. The glacé cherries

of the female host's cheeks swell and he watches the cerulean
glass of her eyes. Maybe she's thinking about her own Vitruvian

lovers. How to understand a woman's thoughts? Their penumbra
complexities. You can't. Onwards they go, into the tundra.

*

They repeat the year of her death as though it were ancient history.
A corpse is under the jurisdiction of personal property rights, apparently.

Rowan Evans

from **On Ēglond**

I

Listen.

It's as if someone offers you a message.
Do you receive me?

The transmission interrupted by crows,
growing dark bristles and claws.

The song swallowed by a sinkhole,
then thrown up after centuries
as mutterings of a bog-queen.

The dispatch intercepted by a cold wind,
snagged on too many thorns.

Torn up, chewed on, translated, left for dead.

Gehȳrest þū?

/ they told you you were singing

/ they told you you were wandering round chambers of the caves
   at dawn

/ they told you you've grown old

/ they told you someone else is occupying your bed

/ they told you nothing except departure

/ they told you day is an outbreak

/ they told you 3 and 6 and 9 and 9

/ they told you many hardships, all that was taken hold of

/ they told you fucking oak trees

/ they told you the loathsome one, who travels on the earth

/ they told you you were the missing chapter from a lost epic

/ they told you you were a dog in a riddle

/ they told you you *were* the riddle

/ that's not what the crow told you

/ how can you misspell a name when you don't have any letters

/ the past is on fire and you are running from it

/ running with it

/ when a hard wind blows they'll know where you've been

IV

Listen:

weder
hwæþre
whether
weather

Wulfes ic mīnes wīdlastum   wēnum dogode.

You're dogged by thoughts of a path,
a track that's wide and lasting.

Routes tug at you like sorrow,
roads outgrow you
þonne hit wæs rēnig weder   ond ic rēotugu sæt.

Where's the short-wave radio,
the meat sandwich, the bag of wood?

You're up a ramshackle tower
hounded by a thought.

Looking for *wræclāsts*.
Looking for wolf-paths   winding and *wendan*.

You've gone rogue, wandering
round waste-ground near a factory.
Reading the map right to left
then left to right, miles from the ringroad.

Looking for flood-paths.
Looking for byways   wet and *biworpen*.

Saying, 'I'm at the gate and I'm here to tear things apart.'

They said, 'be warned, those who will themselves to darkness.'
They said, 'be thankful, those who remain.'
You said, 'it's raining, get the shovel.'

Everything starts to reach and waver.

V

The poem I hold in my hand is a single island,
a stone dropped in a river eleven centuries ago.

Shining, smoothed, altered by water.

It is also amorphous, a stringy mass of texts, pretexts,
limbs, voices, heads, manuscripts, contested grounds, false
    lineages.

Both the stone and sinewy leviathan are true.
They face each other across a pool of liquid.

What is my relation to the stone and to the creature?

Holder, Guardian, Adversary, Child.

Put down the stone, it is burning in your hand.

I offer it to the creature, who holds the stone in its jaws.

A crow hijacks the stillness high above.

There is only a series of instances, a trail of sandbars
dissolving as quickly as they form.

I hold the stone above the sand. There is a deep reflection.
I say something stony, like 'this must be it.'

The many-armed and many-headed.

Oh look, here comes humankind
ready to *geblǣd* on the daisies,
       geblǣd in the hallway,
       geblǣd all over the door.

Its *bitre* encampments *beweaxne* with briars,
the overgrown command.

They told you they couldn't read what you were saying,
because your sentences were full of thorns.

They told you your friends were all *on eorþan*.
Is that 'friends *upon* the earth' or 'friends *within* the earth'?

Making tracks or buried?
Which way is south?

They told you the wreckage of a journey.
They told you '*ic ne mæg*'.

Oh look, here comes the bloody cavalry
saying to a body, 'let me in,'
pounding at the skull, 'let me in.'

How 'gift' held too long
in someone else's mouth
becomes 'sacrifice'.

How 'group' becomes 'threat'.

How 'greet' becomes 'kill'.

How words
tear their wing-bones
and grow new heads
in the wound.

Safiya Kamaria Kinshasa

Gully

Riding the bacterium causing tonsilitis in William Wilberforce's throat,
1689, 1789

a, red, and, whip, man, strip, a, gul, ly, from, my, gul, let,
my, voice, would, run, dat, way, tru. tru. tru, de, mud, de,
gunk, when, mas, sa, came, he, came, at, night, he,
would, press, his, choke, tuh, my, ear, i, was, a, low, tide,
i, tried, tuh, hack, his, his, what, do, you, call, dis, part,
ah, man, dat, em, balm, me? my, toe, nails, grew, night,
fall, my, hole, wide, ned, as, he, punched, with, his, with,
his, liz, ard, tast, ed, like, brine, my, voice, ran, but, ne,
ver, get, far, it, tried, tuh, jump, off, de, edge, ah, east,
but, he, al, ways, find, it, vis, its, me, ag, ain, and, steals,
an, ud, dah, gul, ly, his, his, his, his, sho, vel, bit, de,
right, side, ah, my, neck, my, knuc, kles, lob, bied, ag,
ainst, de, dig, ging, but, im, go, deep, in, my, rib, den,
strip, my, gul, ly, like, im, strip, my _ my,
sir, you, claim, tuh, want, all, ah, we, wid, dout, we, soft,
parts, bound, up, in, a, cart, but, you, say, man, say, man,
say, man, say, man, say, man, ag, ain, im, make, hol, low,
un, der, my, blouse, i, shrunk, seek, ing, and, push, ing, i,
am, sure, i, made, a, noise, i, doan, tink, wun, na, heard,
or, yuh, heard, but, doan, know, what, i, said, i, said,
,   ,   , i, said   ,   ,   ,   ,   ,   ,   ,   ,
,   ,   ,   , sir, can, you, re, peat, what, i, said?
wid   me   crouch   ing   in
your   gul   let

41

'Avoid Direct Contact With the Skull'

– British Natural History Museum

according to How To Get A Man Dot Com,
when a man licks his lips multiple times, pupils
darting from your eyes to lips to chest to womb
it means he wants to frog you, elongate his tongue,
yank your nipples from their lily-pads
then claim you for five minutes, or however less,
no account is made for curious men
who want to know if the rumours are true,
if women like me really do have
big fat spines to carry maps.
while we lay living,
i noticed the way he quarried
me from behind, sex is a strange activity,
weirder when i see it done by people who look like me,
directed by people who don't,
i saw an aunty's skull in a glass case,
a corridor from the ape section,
the glass was valued for more than the skull,
it's only a matter of time before they learn we have more
things to stick on skewers, i am tired my love, i am
oh so tired, my instincts tell me we are not made of war
yet in two thousand nine hundred & twelve years
they will dig up our knees & say we used them
as shanks, if you would like to claim some
part of my skeleton, do not put me on display,
or follow instructions

Momtaza Mehri

Fluke by Any Other Name is a Flight Number

when they first came over nobody knew what Finland was or where it was or
what to even wear on the flight you passed the medical examination & stood
there glorious as a beggar as the Amreekan doctor laughed after the HIV test
& said *you're good to go* next thing you know frost knocks wind from chests &
they're in Tampere home of the swollen-bellied & coincidentally where on a
crisp December mid-morning much like the day of their arrival Lenin first met
Stalin at a Bolshevik conference which is neither here nor there but more press-
ingly is not where they would rather be if given the choice which is unlikely
considering the oceanic gulf between choice & options between affection &
affect put another way on arrival they still couldn't locate their new home on
a map Finnair could only do so much despite regularly being ranked as one of
the safest operating airlines with its last fatal accident occurring in 1963 the
year of Diet Coke & four little girls & Malcolm's body in Michigan his spirit in
Bandung in Nairobi in Paris in Saigon *don't be shocked when I say I was in prison
you're still in prison that's what America means prison* oh for such delicious clar-
ity the warm butter of his rage a speech later sampled by Public Enemy then
recycled as part of the soundtrack to the video game *Sonic Rush* a cobalt blue
& white hedgehog the same colour of the Finnish flag a force unable to catch
up with itself the perfect metaphor for modernity & the ache of a wrist held
in anticipation for the conveyer belt to return their luggage if not their coun-
try both will do both they carry on their shoulders

but only one will weigh them down

On Memory as Molasses as Muscle as Miasma

in the old country Khadija drives a Fiat Mirafiori
full-bellied & often faulty
gas from each of its mouths   like a preacher
a cassette case lies gutted   in the glovebox
sets scratchy funk to motion
brakes grunt between her legs   she is an educated woman
the first to leave & begin elsewhere
watch her catholic schoolgirl dreams ripen
her mother is older than her own country
to be a child of such fictions is to live   fossilised in amber
look   how well she wears these myths
of borders & beginnings   like silk shawls
somewhere between a minaret   & the Arch of Umberto
fascism is just another bridge you innocently walk under
here   in this lamented age   before Kasarani
before Lampedusa   before collapse & containment
before diaspora & dispersal before the Mediterranean claimed us
    as her favourites
before the burst of waters & bonds

each morning she dabs her wrists   with a drop of lilac
invents a regime of her own
at their houses she wipes a table clear   adjusts her apron
on hands and knees   she reaches the furthest crevices
fluffs one pillow after another   the weight of a silvered tray
                 & an officer's hand
is a daily calculation   sublimate desperation into a wisp of faith
akhirah is the afterbirth   is the afterlife
is the handprint of absence   the officer's hand is the silvered tray
the silvered tray is the officer's hand   both rest warm
against the chest   both feed cousins back in
    the village
she dreams of return   does not know what she will return to

Napoli sighs outside   efficient in its alienation
housewives fling their windows open
cat from the morning's palms   let the breeze swell
let it usher in the kind of promises

                                        a stranger can believe in

Kandace Siobhan Walker

Third Gender Sonnet

Everyone is female and everyone hates it.
          – Andrea Long Chu

Pop girls on the radio are singing about gender.
At the awards shows they are dancing gender.
On the silver screens they are playing gender.
In the high street shops they are buying gender,
drinking gender in the bars, kissing gender in the clubs,
reading gender on the bus to work, drawing gender on
the breath-frosted window with gender's own finger,
leaving the newspaper's front-page gender on the seat.
Landing on 'third gender' on the form with three tickboxes,
no write-in gender, then scribbling out this answer,
crossing out this umbrella gender entirely, picking a tophat
    gender
of the remaining two, incorrect genders, though not equally,
because this is where a third option leads us, gender escapees
    at a canyon
where our gender runs out of road.

Alto

I watch nature documentaries, cancel the doctor's,
listen to Nina Simone 'til my skin turns blue.
The fair packs up for winter, I knead rosaries,
dunk paper wicks in urine with the religion of a rigged game.
Glaciers and species sink into extinction. I have appropriated loss.
Pearls running across my knuckles, mesh of a birdcage
veil brushing my cheeks, I confess: when I was fourteen
I joined the school choir to sing scales with a pretty alto.
We went swimming in our red cassocks, wet hair curling
like tongues folding over crispbread. We didn't need a word for
her hands pulling the white surplice over my head.
We pretended we shared the same escape routes, but
loneliness was easier for her to bear than punishment.
Whenever I prayed to be discovered, she kicked me under the pews.
I don't need to wonder if she has bled as extensively as I have.
At the spring fair I will eat cotton candy, ride the bumper cars
'til I appear in a rose window. There are all kinds of altars,
and there are just as many tables I won't ever name.

The Forward Prize for Best Single Poem –
Written
Shortlisted poems

Kathryn Bevis

My body tells me that she's filing for divorce

She's taken a good, hard look at the state
of our relationship. She knows it's not
for her. The worst thing is, she doesn't tell
me this straight up or even to my face. No.
She books us appointments with specialists
in strip-lit rooms. They peer at us over paper
masks with eyes whose kindness I can't bear.

They speak of our marriage in images:
a pint of milk that's on the turn, an egg
whose yolk is punctured, leaking through
the rest, a tree whose one, rotten root
is poisoning the leaves. I try to understand
how much of us is sick. I want to know
what they can do to put us right. She,

whose soft shape I have lain with every night,
who's roamed with me in rooky woods, round
rocky heads. She, who's witnessed the rain
pattering on the reedbed, the cut-glass chitter
of long-tailed tits, the woodpecker rehearsing
her single, high syllable. How have we become
this bitter pill whose name I can't pronounce?

Soon, she'll sleep in a bed that isn't mine.
That's why, these nights, we perform our trial
separations. She, buried in blankets, eyelids
flickering fast. Me, up there on, no — wait —
through the ceiling, attic, roof. I'm flying, crying,
looking down. *Too soon*, I whisper to her warm
and sleeping form. *Not yet. Too soon. Too soon.*

Malika Booker

Libation

You climb into everlasting and so it begins
ancestor, nine nights of praise, of honour,
white spirits poured into the ground to feed
your thirsty mouth. The sting of alcohol
at the back of your throat. And so, it begins
you join our ancestor's altar. Your existence
now relies on memory and traction. How you
make your displeasure known through dreams
dropping food as it approaches the lips
of the family member's mouth, *feed me*,
you say *we are hungry*, so we create plates
and water, plus candles to light your feast
of favourite food from this short life.
My aunt favoured smoked herring, the salt
of it (like the sea, like the salt of the earth)
with dumpling and hard food. How
we feed you to protect us, age-old customs
slinking through slavery to remain. The
youths might have forgotten every ritual
but remember the classic – to throw spirits
for the soul of their fallen brothers. Even these
killed by the hands of kin, skin black like theirs,
whose lives became full stops, from knives
or gunshots, and today parents bury their young
men. While youths too young to know your ways,
fling down rum, pour whole bottles of spirits
by gravesides, part homage, part ancestral, part
knowing that they could easily be in there,
part thankful for another day. You there
schooling these youth men in how to be ancestors
in the afterlife – there is no language
in the landscape of our ancestors to contend
with all this loss. So, pour the rum, just pour.

Kizziah Burton

Oh Do You Know The Flower Man

He watches flowers. He admires flowers. He draws near flowers.
He tenders flowers. He caresses flowers. He picks flowers.
He weighs baskets of flowers. He weighs my face of flowers.
He offers a night of flowers. He threads a string of flowers
for my door and for my altar. Flowers of devotion. Flowers
for an evening fire. Flowers for a Pluto moon. He lays flowers

across my long bed, my long hair, my longing for him. Flowers
for a collarbone. Flowers for a throat. Until my voice flowers
in this flower dress. This mons of flowers. This cup of flowers,
this perfumed breast, this canticle, this rose cloister of flowers,
this anthologia. He provides moths and bumblebees for flowers.
He provides lemon grass and slender stalks. He strings flowers

through my lily bells and flowerheads of chrysanthemum flowers.
He provides waters drenched in honeycomb. He showers flowers
with kisses, showers of praise – into a breathless litany of flowers.
He says I am the fragrance of hyacinth, the essence of all flowers.
He says I am the fragrance of earth, of rain, of sun, sun flowers,
of musk, of patoulli, oud, and civit. He says, 'with these flowers.'

He proposes flowers. He sews a sash around my waist of flowers.
He provides a ley of huckleberries for my bridlepath of flowers.
He escorts me in a brief pageant of cereus grandiflorus flowers.
He composes eulogies. Says, 'I author you with these flowers.'
He sighs soft falling flowers. Beglamours my speechless flowers.
He beguiles me with his dew wet flowers. His eyes of sad flowers.

A looming mist of flowers. Elaborate aching delphinium flowers.
Flowers of misdirection. Rows of trembling paperwhites flower.
He injures me with leaves, with grasses, slant stems of flowers.
He destroys me with seeds, roots, rhizomes – with riling flowers,
masses of memoried flowers, ruptured petals. Veiled in flowers,
he turns them into extending, rounded violent equations of flowers.

He extends the lengthy verse needling nipples pink with flowers.
He says, 'I stay you with flowers, a shrine of flowers.' Wildflowers.
He hems my mouth shut in flowers. Lengthens my neck in flowers.
A long daisy chain of flowers. Swaying me above heirs of flowers.
He encircles the throats of my wrists in lianas of clematis flowers.
He stems me in a chassis of tallow for cold enfleurage. Flowers

lay across my long bed of earthlace in fields of ashphodel flowers.
Or he merely continues to tease petals from my lost bits of flowers.
Or at night he urges quince thorns into my laurel wreath of flowers.

Breda Spaight

The Curse

My father slathers the vulva
with lubricant, the fat lips glossy
as a chestnut, while my brother holds the tail
from which clinkers of dried shit dangle,
her ginger flank also matted in shit. She stands
in the cattle crush, head clamped in the bail,
looking like a tourist admiring the view
through the open window of a train, as though
her head has nothing to do with her body
and her body is all about what she carries,
as my father grasps and grapples with the slithery, banana
-yellow hooves spreading the vulva, as only the vulva can
spread, flap to the world girdled in fibres spun to burn;
my brother holding the tail's butt now, raising it up as my father
nooses the calf's legs with ropes, first one, then the other,
naked to the waist, glimmer of mushroom-white flesh
in the February light of the barn; my brother, like a
referee in a boxing match, shuffles close to the action
as though he has done this for all the twelve years of his life,
born to it, born to do, to be, the man in his voice the day he curses
me for losing his blue marble, *I hope you've twins,*
four of them, all in one go! My body already a future
to fear, blood that's not stopped by a cold key; sorrow
and dread that I'll be a woman. The vulva pulses its signal
for my father to pull; arched back, neck, head, arms
racked, feet rooted to the ground for traction, ropes
wound through bloodless fists, the vulva
like the mouth of a child spewing; remnants
of the water sac drool like dribble, as if she's drunk,
as though she sings this new life into the world.
The vulva drawn now to its polished unwrinkled purity,
the last fierce fibres suctioning out what longs for life;
the calf's snout, eyes, ears framed in an umber aureole,

its rude, puce tongue, its tawny body a bag of bones
as it tumbles to the ground and steams; my father breathless,
hands on his hips, my brother his mirror
as they stand over all creation.

Eric Yip

Fricatives

To speak English properly, Mrs. Lee said, you must learn
the difference between *three* and *free*. Three men
escaped from Alcatraz in a rubber raft and drowned
on their way to Angel Island. Hear the difference? Try
this: you fought your way into existence. Better. Look
at this picture. Fresh yellow grains beaten
till their seeds spill. That's threshing. That's
submission. You must learn to submit
before you can learn. You must be given
a voice before you can speak. Nobody wants to listen
to a spectacled boy with a Hong Kong accent.
You will have to leave this city, these dark furrows
stuffed full with ancestral bones. Know
that death is thorough. You will speak of bruised bodies
skinnier than yours, force the pen past batons
and blood, call it fresh material for writing. Now
they're paying attention. You're lucky enough
to care about how the tongue moves, the seven types
of fricatives, the articulatory function of teeth
sans survival. You will receive a good education
abroad and make your parents proud. You will take
a stranger's cock in your mouth in the piss-slick stall
of that dingy Cantonese restaurant you love and taste
where you came from, what you were made of all along.
Put some work into it, he growls. *C'mon, give me
some bite*. Your mother visits one October, tells you
how everyone speaks differently here, more proper.
You smile, nod, bring her to your favourite restaurant,
order dim sum in English. They're releasing
the students arrested five years ago. *Just a tad more
soy sauce please, thank you.* The television replays
yesterday on repeat. The teapots are refilled. You spoon
served rice into your mouth, this perfect rice.
Steamed, perfect, white.

Highly Commended Poems

AJ Akoto

Daughterhood

No one had ever told her
the possibility of undaughterhood.
Or how the weight of mothers
can be shrugged off —
not like a coat but
like the rolling stone of a sepulchre,
hard at first, then easier with the inertia,
and then a last flick.

No one had told her that she could be good
and undutiful at the same time.
Oh, she thought, if I ever
have a daughter, I will tell her
that she can be free of me.
Perhaps that way she won't want to be,
but if she does, I'll know
the brightness of having told her
that such a wonder exists.

Anthony Anaxagorou

Float

The chance to be part of this happens briefly:
my son grows to edge where the ocean slips, roughly
pointing towards a float,   he asks
me to rescue it from a future he can't see –
three slow steps in until I'm governed by cold
moving towards an unknown confluence. I'll say

how I panickcd, unmoored by my weight. they say
the closer you get to time the further it moves, for a brief
second I believed I could make a difference, another cold
thought splits my side   salt clings, feels rough
around my limits, each wave dumping sweat. I see
my son's worry in the surge, hear his asking

rumble through the earth's bladder, I want to ask
for more time. how can a body reverse in water? I say
aloud *I don't think I'll make it*   seeing
his profile plunge like a conch. as a boy I took a brief
diving course where I learnt how oxygen turns starfish rough
drying them into land until a child discovers the cold

of them, chucking what's left into a bucket. over time our colder
selves arrive to find us struggling against the drift, asking
for a cup of moonlight to sunny the medals from our rougher
years.   say
I persevered, not wanting him to see me fail, even if for a brief
second he lost sight of me or believed I drowned at sea –

I'll stay repurposing my strongest lines, see
the float reaching for my hand, the gap becoming less cold,
reminding me the ocean is alive inside the world; its brief
to keep the retina saline, to not need a question, asking
for little in return. the sea: it refuses to say
why it keeps down the masthead, the ghost roughly

the size of my son's waiting. I turn towards him roughly
where I left, what's keeping me afloat? my work sees
him dressing up for a life, rehearsing what I'll finally say
hill-walking out the ocean his float in hand, juddering from cold
I did it for you   I'll declare   if he ever asks
where I was the whole time then I'll keep my explanation brief

roughly the way my father did during those colder years
when I begged his hand to turn me calm. I'm looking across the
    foreshore.
I can't see him anywhere. I had this to give. to say briefly.

Vicci Bentley

The Policeman's Daughter

after Paula Rego

Good girls love their fathers if
they know what's good for them.

The room sweats. She can smell his acrid sleep.
The cat frets at the door, claws for midnight.

His empty jacket restrains a chair back,
black jack boots stand to attention in the corner.

One by one, she takes them onto her clean white
lap, fist fucks them to her armpits, spits

buffs filth and blood from the caps to such brilliance
she sees her face.

Tara Bergin

In hindsight it strikes me as odd that when X mistook my tenderness for sadism I didn't think 'he's misunderstood me' but rather 'he's seen something I didn't know was there'.

Penetration

Liz Berry

Eliza

Queen of all wet-the-beds and dander,
common nettles and dock,
sticklebacks, angle shades, sparrows, lice,
moles hung from nails like velvet gloves.
In the lezzer beyond the cut, see her –
queen of dung beetles and dog violets,
a crown on her head of all the town's daisies,
grime on their petal tips. Eliza
pursing her lips to a grass-blade,
calling up its music: come on come up!
The world is too alive to be down
in the dark, too afire, too fledgy.
Eliza's hair, dirty sorrel in sunlight,
lights the long grass ablaze.
Little queen of Fiery Holes,
with her back-to-back court, all its slum
and love, its cram like a burrow.
Eliza, queen of all lowly creeping souls,
all toilers and darklings. All shunned things
lay their blessings
at her wet and holey stockinged feet.
Long live the queen! Happiness is a wind
that whistles straight through.

Laurie Bolger

Parkland Walk

Some tech god has made an app so you can hear birds and name them
the police helicopter is going so   we speak loud
the broken bird box is left hanging but they're still going
some woman told me and Hannah not to come down here on our own
don't go down there on your own girls and if you do for god's sake stay together –
Hannah lost her Dad last month so I am chirping at her about a place for us to get
good spaghetti
there's a snail right in the middle of things
its shiny trails are like rain caught in a spider's web
the bin has shit all over the path again
someone has graffitied a sun onto the side of the big trunk in a mess of yellow
so the bark is like the potatoes we dipped in paint and dragged around the plate
     when we were small
a jogging man is convinced that the wedding proposal is just right
and the locals have had time to draw sad faces on all of the stumps
a little girl's dad chases her along the path
I make a joke about the woman with the warning I wanted to say
my legs are thick with blood and yes they can   *run*
                              I learnt to ride a bike on a path just like this one

I got too wide for the slide
I made perfume in milk bottles from petals for all of the mums
who told us not to go too far

I ask Hannah *what do you need girl?* – and she says she won't remember any of
     this in grief
     it's like Sally said just walk with her for now and so we walk into the trees

Chen Chen

The School of Australia

Your emergency contact has called
to quit. Your back-up plan has backed
away. Your boyfriend has joined a boy band
named All Your Former Boyfriends

& Sarah McLachlan. In the ugly
teapot/uglier luggage section of your local
Dillard's, you would like to scream.
Meanwhile, your father has decided

to pursue his original dream & move
to Australia, the brochure version he fell for
in college. In Australia, he will study Beach
Studies & his Western name *Tony*

will finally catch on. *Tony,*
the Australians will say, *where have they been hiding
you?* & Tony will say, *I never imagined I'd be doing
way better than my son.* & on his way home

from the school of the beach, its shells & endless
glitter, Tony will toss out a dog-eared copy
of the manual he received upon arriving in America—
How to Have Deeply Sorrowful Exchanges

with Your Son About Your Immigrant Hardships:
How to Make Him Understand He Must Become
a Neurosurgeon/At Least a Dentist.
The manual will go on to a second career

titling academic papers.
Australia will be renamed Tony's
Son Get Your Shit Together!
TSGYST!

will call to say, *But
remember? You're already a glittery stretch
of dream. Your own
emergency Tony.*

Geraldine Clarkson

Leperskin Coat

When I awoke, he was wearing his
leperskin coat, an elbow out
at the left, a wrist at the right, and
holes for England in his endless seams,
all for pity's sake.

I was used to his wiles, his Wednesday
face, wild 'clean-me' eyes, but this,
this.

Bleach, I said.

When you know someone's trying to force
your affection with cadaver-chic, and your heart's
half that way anyway but
you're not going to be made love's
fool forever. Victim to a pinch-me penchant.

He hangs a high-arm gap near to your lips,
your tongue could once-round it as quick as talk.
It looks salt. *Use bleach*, you repeat

but you're lost, his holes and cavings
calling you, unavoidable voids, violet
scrimshaw trouble, slinky invisible

vim, voile negativa, dripping
mangold, and any more than this

is always less.

Rishi Dastidar

from Pretanic: The Brexit book of the dead

Because that's what this is,
that's what we're writing
within this geopolitical Bardo
where we – sorry, a decisive

majority of us – has decided
that nostalgia is the best form
of statecraft to respond to a
future of heatproof algorithms

fighting wars that the humans
don't survive. I believed it
once too, that currency unions
decay but nations never die,

that subsidiarity was a theory
never tested, that the *acquis*
was common the way silk
handcuffs are. But then war

never killed our glory, and we
were never de-illusioned, just
disillusioned – why can't we
play the Blitz every week please?

So now we wait outside this
Berlaymont purgatorio,
dreaming of lions swimming
across la Manches, unicorns

conquering continents, the people's
bloodhounds chasing complexity's
fox. Look! we have Dover's
liberating cliff edge coming up,

because we are never freer
than when we are falling to
victory over the imperial lorry
park formerly known as Kent –

and is that RMS Dambusters we
see gunning towards the fishing
fields? To bellow and buccaneer
hotly is the only way to die, chums!

In the next place, the cherries
are there to be picked, and the
sound of Lord North squealing,
'Lads, someone's fucked up

more than me!' is sweet nectar
to Empire 2.0, and we forget
that the answer to the question is:
the dead are perfectly sovereign.

Akwaeke Emezi

Disclosure

when i first came out i called myself bi a queer tangle of free-form
dreads my mother said i was sick and in a dark place my father
said i would get AIDS my father-in-law stopped speaking to me
my marriage had been folded open its spine cracked my husband
returned to snow in his sinuses my childhood friend screamed over
the phone *what was the point of getting married* my brother said you
can't live in that bubble in new york the real world is not like that
but it's a lie there are no real worlds you can live in whatever
bubble you like a diving bell made of tender glass clap your hands
if they said you're too sensitive if they beat you because they could
because you should be tougher harder gra gra ghen ghen an igbo
man in my friend's home laughs and holds my food out of reach i
am so tired my friend holds me in the bathroom as i cry the next
day he apologizes says he likes my name but he'll never give it to
his daughter because he wants her to be strong not like me i don't
tell him how little he matters how i have his type at home how they
already raised me with blows across the face a belt in a doorway a
velvet child upholstered in incoherent rage one day a coward who
will break my heart asks me how i ended up still so soft i tell him i
am stubborn i wanted a better world a diving bell made of tender
glass a better family i remembered how to be a god i give myself
what i want no one raises their voice in my house no one lays their
fleshy hands on me no one is cruel if they are fool enough to try
then they die and what a death what a death to not be loved by
me anymore the softest gate-opener i feast on torn herbs and fat
gold the wet smear of a perfect yolk seeds burst purple beneath
my hands a pulped satsuma bleeds dark juice into my mouth who
knew i could love me so loudly who knew i would survive who
knew their world meant nothing meant nothing meant nothing
look when i last came out i called myself free.

Katie Farris

In the Early Days of a Global Pandemic

In the early days of a global pandemic
I can't stop writing about love, while everyone

is writing about a country.
Everywhere in America (is everywhere

America, yet?)—in America,
which is to say, everywhere—

Americans are spreading rumors,
<u>writing</u> about a country as if a country existed

in the midst of a global pandemic, about its citizens
as if we were visible, while America, which is an idea

in our grasp, twists itself into an eagle,
condenses into a bowl of hot chicken soup,

then a factory never retrofitted to make ventilators, then a trillion
dollars, then fresh water, then saltwater,

then salt.

Salena Godden

While Justice Waits

there they go again
filling your mouth
with their name

there they go again
adding more weight
to your burden

there they go again
giving you all the anxiety
whilst telling you not to panic
when the panic is deeply rooted in
centuries of ... there they go again

there they go again
contradicting their own rules
double speak and double standards

there they go again
your dead are statistics
your ghosts live in hashtags

there they go again
getting away with murder
but calling it anything else

there they go again
doing nothing
as your vulnerable
and sick and dying
need all your love and care
and your living need all of your
focus, energy and time

there they go again
filling your plate
with their jobs
and the work
they should do
as your elected leaders

there they go again,
dominating your thoughts
so no work can get done

there they go again
grimacing on the front page
hogging the limelight
with this theatre of
performative cruelty

there they go again
suffocating light and hope
like a pillow held fast over the face
of the kicking and struggling truth

there they go again
consuming all the oxygen
and rewriting history

there they go again
like it's all about them
but it is because of them
and it is in spite of them

there they go again
obscuring the facts
blurring the edges
blinkering the horse
filtering the picture

there they go again
there they go again
there they go again

and it is not the names of the dead
nor the name of the nurse
not the name of the innocent
but their name in your mouth

how can it be?
that when you wake in the night
wailing and mourning and hurting
they are marching on your tongue
they are renting your insomnia

there they go again
using your anguish as garnish
using your defence as an attack
using your fear to divide you
using your rage to pass draconian laws
using your pain to sell shit back to you
using your grief to decorate newspapers
using your anger to kill you

because there they go again
casting an ass in the lead role
the wealthy politicians in the spotlight
the hideous clown gets top billing
the monster as the headline act

your horror gets a walk on part
your mourning cries are extras
your fury is the chorus line
your humanity the supporting cast

while justice waits in the wings

Em Gray

Symbiosis

I've seen a horse
take the soft folds of a dog's scruff
between her corn kernel teeth.

He, quite forgetting the bones of himself,
dangled some seconds
before being lowered down.

The care of that horse
as if she were practised in placing
chandeliers, or weighing sacks of truffles
with her mouth

and how the dog paused
as if to reassure the horse
of no awkwardness between them
after that solemn transaction of theirs

in which (I like to think)
no liberties were taken
save a horse who wished
a moment's velvet on her grassy tongue,
an old dog's wish to float.

Elle Heedles

Rain Noise

in the courtyard. There is rain
and there are stars. The rain collapses

through the tannins. I follow the reflection
of rain in the window of tenderness,

chase it through the trees to find someone
with your particular eyelashes. I will keep everything

someone could want: the cold, shade,
the vamp that plays on the hour, this unbelievable letter.

When the swings scrape in the wrong key, it is time to go home.
I tear a name from the middle part where the ducks swim.

I have mistaken you for sky, for waterfalls, but never
for an animal of stars. That is me. Echoes

from every corner. The dog
looks at me sideways. What did he make

of us that night, when I was a silver tooth,
a touch in time, and you the view

from the window, the grass under the needles.
All day the dog waits for a hymn from the pines.

The rain carries wishes
from the sky down.

Selima Hill

People in Taxis

She puts – she *pops* – her finger on my nose –
the 'button nose' that makes me so adorable,
so like a little pug, or pig, or piglet;

she thinks it's just so yummy she could chew it –
as soft as cheeks, as chubby as tomatoes,
as puppy fat that's begging to be nuzzled;

she can't resist feeding me with sugar-lumps
while those who are less fond of *helping others*
glide about the capital in taxis.

Emma Jeremy

i talk about the beach

on the beach today it's snowing
and i'm asking now
to be there
my skin dipping in and out of the water
all cold and alive
in a way i don't feel guilty for
at night i'm struggling
staying in my body is difficult
in my dreams i'm under tables
looking up at myself eating dinner
or under my own bed
looking up at myself sleeping
my shoes never on me
and their absence having an important meaning
which is that i'm unable to stand
that i'm always underneath something
looking up or sitting on a ground
which is wet with not snow or sand or salt water
while my real body exists somewhere else
like alongside my friends
sitting around a table
all of them laughing because
nothing's happened to them yet
my body laughing because
without me it can
and when my friends then stand up
to leave the table they're sharing
i know things are beginning to change
and i know this is happening
because i recognise it as the thing i fear
so i watch my friends becoming good fathers
my friends building homes for themselves
my friends sleeping well in large comfortable beds

while i have to climb through
everything that needs to be climbed through
to get back to my body which
as i've said before
should be on that beach

Majella Kelly

Forget

Forget the Memorial Garden. It doesn't know
what it's supposed to remember. Could it be connected
to the name of the town: Tuaim = tumulus = burial ground?

Never mind. Was it for famine victims when it was a workhouse?
Or soldiers when it was a barracks? Or maybe the Mothers
and Babies when it was their Home? No.

What kind of home has high walls topped with broken glass?
Forget the Memorial Garden. It can't remember its secret
chambers, once used for sewage, remembers less the seven hundred

and ninety-six missing children. All that's on its mind today
is the thrush's nest in the Guelder Rose (which, by the way, knows
it isn't really a rose), and what haunts the garden most

are the blunt ends of the blue-green eggs. Will there be enough
air for the chicks to breathe before they break their shells?

Victoria Kennefick

SUPER KING

There is a corpse on our bed.
It is Jesus, down from the cross,
the blood spattered across
his rippling torso, the crown of thorns
ripping the pillow slip and the flesh
on his forehead. I don't know why
He is here, with *that* heart
exposed, His eyes
closed. He *is* dead,
I think. But you know how men
can be, they say
one thing, and the next thing you know
they're on the road
showing off their open wounds
while back at home
the women weep.

Karl Knights

The Night Before My PiP Tribunal I See My Dead

You left a note.
'Please don't judge me
too harshly.' I read it
at your memorial.
I hate that my voice
didn't shake.
Your mum worried
she'd broken your knees
when she cut you down.
When your dad scattered
your ashes pieces of you
flew back in his face.
You starved to death.
At the inquest
the embalmer said
it was obvious
you died in agony.
When your sister heard that
she went straight to the bar.
Three years' sobriety gone.
Your funeral was the worst.
It was just me, your gran,
the hired pallbearers
and the priest, who kept
thumbing his gown.
Bailiffs found your body.
Your cat was screaming,
they said. You were so thin.
They slid bags of sand
into your casket
so we could feel the weight
on our shoulders.
You would have

liked the crowd,
the thick procession
of callipers, canes, crutches.
The relatives always asked me
to speak. I was the writer,
I'd know what to say.
So many dead,
so many of my dead. After
twenty-seven funerals, I stopped
counting. At the last one
I held myself up
at the pulpit,
got through the usual words.
Faces like tea-bags
left out to dry looked back
at me. Sitting outside the church
we talked about your favourite
party trick, opening beer bottles
with your wheel spokes.

Zaffar Kunial

Empty Words

'they may not acorde' –
Chaucer's *Assemble of Foules* –
Parliament of Words.

*

The Speaker's habit
prolongs a vowel: 'The *aye*s have
it. The *aye*s have it.'

*

I would not accuse
anyone of misreading
big vowels like *Us*.

*

Clanging the zen gong –
is it ego, that I add:
Something keeps going

*

My father's Kashmir
ended with a smoky sigh –
its long rhyme with here.

*

Onland – opposite
of Offland. The capital
is shared, disputed.

*

Long hush. A good shout.
Give me this wait. Not the screen's
stone-cold OUT / NOT OUT.

*

Kant's *crooked timber* –
cricket bats can be English
or Kashmir willow.

*

In the beginning –
that middle was the spark – *or*
was the *Word*'s Big Bang.

*

Dad's word for 'and': *aur*.
More like *oar* – than *our* – as in
out at sea. And *or*.

*

Near Lahore, Dad's eye,
through smashed specs, met a firework.
Near Gloucester, King Lear.

*

Classic. Thought we'd be
a *Ulysses*, not, instead
'The Dead'. Long story.

*

Mr Palomar –
wore specs, like the deep space lens
flecked by dust and stars.

*

The Rat's small minute –
live 'By it and with it and
on it and in it'.

*

Prayer is not the words
but having none and staying.
Bell-less fairy weed.

*

look, love – a foxglove
hear the bee that hums within –
the *be* in forgive

Nick Laird

Talking to the Sun in Washington Square

Looking after children means simultaneously building a field hospital,
a hedge school, a diner and an open-air prison with your bare hands
and operating them at a continual loss. In this instant they are playing

and you're sitting on a bench where the sun applies itself to the square
and you can feel it on your skin asking how it's been since you last touched,
and you tell her things are alright mostly, the sky is the epitome of sky,

the clouds give birth to themselves, the little people are getting even better
at belittling the bigger people, and you are done in now. You did your bit.
Birdwatching today in Central Park until you saw an osprey with a fish

in its beak and a splinter in a finger meant you had to all walk out and hail
a cab, and you saw the booth on sixth had its phone yanked off and wires
dangled. It took you to the endless conversation at dinner last night

about silence where your wife mentioned John Cage and the persistence
of absence in presence, or something, and the Mexican writer recited the noun
for quiet in four languages and you said nothing, offering, you thought,

the most evincive contribution. Now the sun is trying to tell you something
by splitting through the cloud like that. Some secret as to how its light
walks and flies at the same time, or why the nature of formations – clouds,

crowds, poems, marriage – is that they dissolve, and why there is such
an effort in just not. Heaven is a past participle of heave, the sun notes,
and the fountain stands to attention until she sets and it slumps to the pool.

You'd like to hear more about that sometime but not quite yet. You want
to know if all lives viewed from the inside present as a series of failures.
You want the side door held ajar a moment longer. This is the permacrisis,

sun. It is grim, the era of collapsing systems, of gaming the algorithm,
of the discontent late capitalism must inflict on us for it to thrive.
What you want is old friends who admit to complications not followers

or allies. The instantaneous personal magnetism of other people
is almost overwhelming sometimes – attractive or repelling.
The sun rests its hand on you and everyone and says, very softly,

Look how my light alights on the rock dove and the litter bin alike,
useless to corporations, meeting the froth of the cottonwood,
the bespectacled pianist, interstitial fauna, the angry kings of meth,

lovers solving the crossword, a Chinese student quietly crying,
all varying configurations of the code, and wait until I disappear
before you wander back in the way that fire wanders to make

an early dinner and clean up, bath the children and tell them stories.

Vanessa Lampert

Tower

My father took me to London
when my whole fist could fit
inside his palm.

On the tube he lifted me up
and, holding tight stepped out
from our carriage to the next
through the filthy hurtling dark
to thrill me, then did it again.

By the river he bought chestnuts
roasted on a brazier.

My red gloves swung on strings.
I looked up at the tower of him,
and grief would never dare
to touch my life.

Fran Lock

Of Familiars/I Shall Go Into a Hare

this time it's true: no bourgeois *sozialer mord*. those *early and unnatural deaths* belong to you. fear us. fear us as you fear the crowd, the curse, the reeking incursions of disease. at the sight of us, your metaphors turn vermin. my dear *el presidente*, my dear elite, and all you fickle dreamboats of soft power, please. didn't you know? we spread by ripple and resonance – a rumour in your campaign prosodies. this time it's true: *evil* is *éveil*, to wake, arouse, to rouse, a ruse. ours is nightjar, nightjeer. jaw-jacked, jackdawed sky and us a swoon of birds, a sleeve of snakes. say us names: *malkin*. *vinegar tom*. sing *sack & sugar*, knit their wingspans into flight with fear. ours is cheap hashish and myrtle, myrrh's sweetest chervil murmur. attrition's stink. atonement's smoke. oracles of coronach: grief's gracious policy. knives jostle. our bladed laurels. adepts, nurses, we. thieves of thyme. of sorrel. of medlar's fuckpad mufti, the hedgerow's corpsy lore. we've hagtaper bullock's bane, a penny pricksong, lugs and worts. hey you, whoreson, sawbones, hawthorn suck. we're out for you. boil the bloodshot eyebright up, and sing us cunt a velvet thug. teased thread and bitten thumb. this time it's real. *all* of us witches. inflame your vacant stare with blutwurz, lobes of tormentil. tormented vessels burst. a bitter pill, a split lip, spill a saucer of sour milk. beat and fold a hex until it forms its stiff white peaks of s l o w poison. sloe gin. slurring low. *pyewacket & pigwiggen*, sing. *holt*. this halting site, this halting states. the man himself comes conjuredust and cortisone. silver thaler, cimaruta. talismen, us invisible friends. a kiss lands and a black spot blossoms. blots the sun. ours the incurable noose, the ducking stool, the stake, the brick through the window, the weight of a bull's balls swollen with blood, a letterbox gagging on petrol. anonymous hatemail, and *all* of us witches. thin as a crease in a dirty sheet. baby mama. scrape-backed ponytail, a whip without a hand. wiping a scream on your cheek. how a scream is a yawn with the sound turned up. we're tired of you, you sun-kissed kings of cancer, you courtesans of arcade fire and eye-fuck. us do the dryhump and the mandrake, and so many lovers. go blighted, lisping, stitch us shut. we trade in knots and scalps. slashed achilles, smithereens, moodswings, rings, miscarriages. in incantations, withering. call us *skadi*, scald-crow, backslang and axehead, the larynx crushed. the moon through all its deep throat phases, featherglide deluxe. we spit you back at you through the sewer of our saying. fatten the chattels, reprise your fire. it's real this time. we're with baba yaga. with pendle's tethers, the slings and arrows of islandmagee. we are with gowdie and chattox and dunbar. we are with lorde and with valerie solanas. we are with witches. all of us witches. the underworld attends us. buried at a crossroads, delivered to the compass, delivered of a rabbit, of a foreclosed farm, a ruined church. our slant and split-foot operatives. their luckless delving rue. sieve the breath for nails. provocateurs: black calabash, black bowl, black drum. black bow, black hole, black gold. we know what we owe. the weeping yew, the slaughtered ewe, the warm embraceable you. watch us like an old maid playing patience, frail and sly. we peel our sleeves, reveal a ladder. we peel ourselves, revealed, reviled. this revelry, this reveille of skin. sing *elemanzer, peckin the crown*. drown, father-fucker. cat-shapes sit on babychests: *mačka*, the *marime*-most part of being. us straddle the bright air, piss standing up. where a foul mouth is a souvenir. the human ear, a heresy of pearls. teeth are strewn to hamper harvest. an errand out of ears of corn. sickened calves, a child entangled in a day-glo shriek. your parables and scams. fleece you, of all your moral fables, all your fabled marbles, all your summonses and psalms. oh, us from the mardy vagabondage of bog-places. read your red idea in dregs of cold tea. nettles and infection. *old time religion*. vestments and pedestals. girls grid-locked into girdles, lockstepped into marriage. oh herbicides, the common-law language of flowers, you heterofucks, you herods, you lordlings, your vocation of weeds. remedies, infections, a valkyrie solo for skinning a horse. the razor-tailed magpies. clockworked to conjuries of flight. glove the bone. chew the cud of burdock's false positive. hyssop swig and dittany. tansy, hellebore's ectopic slop. improvise our bridal rorschach one more time. hit us baby, one more time. impressionistic on our bed. the priests' collective guesswork wagging fingers over us. mess, corrective cleansing. whaleboned bursaries of flesh. the pumpkin splits. euphoria, the juices run and london's burning. keep your moon maidens, your swan maidens, soapy-soft and lyre-beguiled. oh, we're not *wiccan*. patchwork and craftfair and potpourri. women's work is gutting fish, whore-toil, endless pussy-craft. all of us witches. sprawling like a midland city. this body washes itself in the body. menstrual scum, ulterior honey, carpal sluts, all of us: rose-chafers, handmaidens, thai brides, bull dykes. the complete girlfriend experience. make scented forfeits from the sunshine. ribs like cattle grids, our eyebrows meet in the middle. we'll die. we'd rather die. than give an inch. defect. is the fault and the flight. fuck you. this be the night. fuck you.

Adam Lowe

Like This (Polari Version)

A translation of Rumi

If an omi pookers you
how the sharp pagament
of all our charvering thirst
will ochy, sally your ecaf
and screech,

'Like this.'

When some cove zitarries
the boldness of the nochy fakement,
clamber with camp
on the roof and hoof
and screech,

'Like this.'

If a sister wants to clock
what fairy is,
or what Gloria's bona ink means,
lean your noggin toward her.
Keep your mush ajax.

Like this.

When some dish cackles the purano
poetry about shrouds
unvasting the lune,
loosen grop by grop the cords
of your robe.

Like this.

If any soap chidders how
Jesse Herself raised
the brown bread,
don't try to explain the kushti.
Kiss me on the oven instead.

Like this. Like this.

When trade pookers what it means
to 'gag for amour', point here.
If she pookers for my height, frown,
and with luppers gauge the space
between the grinzers on your brow.

This tall.

The fairy sometimes leaves
the bod while coming up.
When a gurrl can't imagine
or vada such suchness,
mince back into my latty.

Like this.

When bones moan
to each other in the cottage
cloister, deep in harva,
they're jibbing
our story.

Like this.

I am a volta where fairies live.
Vada into this
deepening azure,
while the becker breathes
the patter flash.

Like this.

When an omie palone
pookers what
there is to do,
sindarry the randall
in his lills.

Like this. Like this.

When she 'arry varries
back from Cruz,
she'll poke just her cap
around the rim
of the jin to shake us

like this.

Arji Manuelpillai

The Expendables

When I remember my father hugging me,
it isn't actually my father hugging me;
it's a movie I saw with Sylvester Stallone.
He's ruffling my hair, launching me up,
telling me not to do something. When I quit
heroin, I didn't exactly quit heroin, more like
saving a seat with a bag down, slipping in
every now and then — methadone, spirits,
TV dinners, YouTube rabbit holes.
My counsellor says I need a new network.
I tell her I have two kids who ignore me —
what else does a man want? Ha ha ha.
I found a flyer, in the margin ads,
some hall in some pebbledash town,
a group of men, some kinda nice,
kinda charming, like this older guy,
buys me a pint, ready salted crisps,
rests his arm on my shoulder,
tells me about last night, after the pub,
they drove the streets till early hours,
spotted a Sikh boy with a local girl,
broke the kid's collar bone. It's just
good to feel part of something.

Joseph Minden

Historiography

Jason taught me everything I know about history. Once, we were at an Albrecht Dürer exhibition: one drawing was haunted by the lines of another. Jason explained how, not having rubbers, draughtsmen such as Dürer would take a sponge and wipe away, imperfectly, the form they wanted to replace; how a trace remained.

Jason moved on to another part of the exhibition and I walked round to the other side of the case to discover that this wasn't true. There was simply another drawing on the reverse side of the paper. I can't remember what either of the drawings were.

Emma Must

from Holloway Letters
(The Martyr's Crown)

for Becca Lush

holloway – lane or path that has been grooved down
into the landscape due to the erosive power of,
variously, feet, wheels and rainwater

[Canerow]

Like the cork oak, in a circle of herself,
each full-grown woman would turn a little girlish
at the prospect of a proper hairdo.

Sitting in lines of three or four, or pairs,
we'd plait each other's hair in tight, flat rows –

part a section to get things started,
make stitch braids out of the strands,
adding in hair from the row below.

We dreamed in parallel:
of fields double dug, rough-hoed by the tiller
then ploughed into kick-waves of keels and furrows …

We'd reach the nape and keep on plaiting,
secure each end with a snap bead, bolo tip or barrette,
our loose braids mirrored as a shoal of minnows.

[Wild]

Our loose braids mirrored as a shoal of minnows,
we'd go to 'Education' in the library
and browse through *De Profundis*
or *The Ballad of Reading Gaol*. You could chat
to Annette Tibbles: in for years for conspiracy
to free caged rabbits, so she got a job
shelving novels and looked after the cats.

Dear Annette, thank you for the Marmite
and that amazing information about
police surveillance tactics. I hope
you are out now, that you live on a farm
somewhere quiet with as many animals
as you care to love, rear, feed,
and as many books as you care to read.

[Shares]

And as many books as you care to read
would not be enough to haggle for a lighter,
which, after tobacco, tops the hierarchy
of tradable prison commodities.
You'd hear tales of a two-day barter:
the swapping of a sweatshirt for a quarter
of a matchstick, split along its length.

I was more than happy to peddle hair gel
for chocolate to eke out the portions
dished up in the small dining hall
on a tray filled with hollows –
supper at four then you'd starve till morning.
We swapped a bit of this for a bit of that,
though some would give anything to exchange futures.

[Home]

Though some would give anything to exchange futures,
we were content in our new, shared cell.
We shunted our metal beds into an 'L'
and pinned up a cutting of the cutting
from the *Guardian* to make it more homely.
We learnt that letters out must be unsealed;
that letters in could be collected at 11.30;
that we got a lot more letters than anyone else.

Letters matter. Once, before our appeal,
I was woken by a face through the grille:
'You're on production.' It disturbed the whole dorm.
In the middle of the night, I got up and packed
and everyone started writing letters home.
I've done my time learning how to write back.

Daljit Nagra

from **Indiom**

Dramatis Personae

Addendum: CHORUS is performed by 50 hijras, third gender, who often speak simultaneously, in deference to the original Greek CHORUS

Canto I

I

PROLOGUE BY SCREENWRITER'S COMPANION

PROLOGUE on Babus & Coolie languages, & how Nissim Ezekiel's poem Goodbye Party for Miss Pushpa T.S., *written in Babu English, caused offence on publication in 1970s India*

Screenwriter's Companion lowers a book & speaks into the camera

Salutations. Hi, I'm sat by greenwood tree in kameez
& jodhpur. I'm sate as Ms Barrett Browning who once say,
she eat, she drink so much of classics from under a tree,
        so much that her head ache!

In this break from my 'eat & drink', our screenwriter ask for ars
poetica to announce her talkie, aka film.
They said, to disclose the gist that might aid the baat – the yarn,
        but in Standard English.

Screenwriter's Companion gulps at the thought of attempting Standard English

But first, I'd mention the Victorians who sought civil
servants to run the Raj – these were Babus; the Coolie was
the skivvy. Today's talkie imagines how their English
        endures in modern verse.

I'm sure you'd also adore knowhow of some lingo terms.
Indioms flow from the mood engagement between English
& Indian. Babu & Coolie are both indioms.
        Babu is eccentric

use of indioms. So high Babu is a lavish play
for least 'actual' speech. Meanwhile, Coolie's an oral record
from the unschooled, & low mix of indioms may embrace
       excessive Indic words.

*Screenwriter's Companion raises their script, clears the throat
then recites an 'ars poetica'*

Monthly poetry groups flourish over world giving best
counsel, inspiration & samosa. Today's writing
group, in March 2020, is no different except
       the hill station setting –

is it in India? These Indic-heritage poets,
of whom but-not-one earn their crust in Ind, gather monthly
from over the globe. This month, they're in Bulbul Hall, which sits
       in the vale – Charsovee.

Today's theme is about a poem published five decade
distant by our 'Englisch Langwidge' poet from Ind, Mr
Nissim Ezekiel, you know him? P.S. quote was made
       by that great pretender

Mr Pound, of Mr Eliot's *Wasteland*. Nissim's lay
was for a fellow of his committee – she was leaving,
back in '70s, for good. Sad story? The lay was gay!
       Beaming Babu English.

'Badmash – his new poem! Is, he think, how we perorate!?'
It's how most felt mocked while sat under punkah, including
the lass in his lines! Today's poets will assess the fate
       of all such corruptings.

Oh so exciting! Will they go cut-throat barrack for high
drama in defence of Babu verse, or troop for groupthink;
a porcupine's test – get close as a hug till the pricks bite
       or, 'let's hold back for quilled

stimulus – we're comrades in one individual soul'.
Furthermore, as I've said, Babus were administrators
nurtured by men from the Atlantic Archipelago.
        These sahibs were masters

of the Babu, the Babu in turn mastered the Coolie.
Dear viewer, to add, please put aside your traditional
& classically trained methods. Our sensibility's
        an odd conceptual

double-helixing of the houses where we take our lease.
Plus our polymaths weren't groomed to speak but to execute
paperwork assisting the Raj. Now if you won't mind, please,
        while young Bodleian dude

sits in the Bodleian – I'll stay out here under greenwood
with this spicy-red book. What is it – is an Indian
elementary reader designed for the use of stud-
        ents in the Anglo-vern

acular school, published in 1877,
writ by Mr A. Woollaston, who famously lobby
against vaccines. His book's not apropos to what you'll learn;
        now, go – watch talkie!

Cameras recede as Screenwriter's Companion continues speaking

Before you go, I'll recite from the primer, but please note
those in heavenly situ often recite back-to-front.
Just for you, I'll recite in the de-rigueur mortal mode
        for a moral once taught.

Screenwriter's Companion recites from the primer

POLITENESS

An officer in battle happening to stoop his head, a cannon-
ball passed completely over it & took off the head of a
soldier who stood behind him. 'You see,' said the officer,
'that a man never loses by politeness.' Anon.

Screenwriter's Companion raises a finger & summons the cameras back

Additional addendum. Are Babus ever modest?
Swell show offs we are for certs always offloading info!
Do not be set off course, but keep pace with our exchanges.
　　Onward Christian pongos!

Selina Nwulu

Lips

At the funeral, mourners said she had her father's lips
as if she'd plucked them from the open coffin and stitched
them to her face. How the lips now puppet the words

it's what he would have wanted despite the storms
in her stomach. How taut to truth they've become.
They will not let her rage speak here. Sorrow knocks

and the lips do not answer. When no one is watching
she peels the lips off her face like skin from a hardened
orange, watching them shrivel and blacken in her palm.

Damen O'Brien

Scene in Medias Res

The frozen present glitters like a frost
full of storefront manikins, poised
between steps, absurd in their candid
frieze, full of fallen things: wine glasses
nudged into suspension, their red tongues
licking air; plates mooned to fracture
and spillage, stiff in their starburst of
spaghetti; a startle of pigeons, lurching
or rising, caught in hard air. I've
wandered these empty full streets, seen
the hot bullets hover, the ball seek its
catcher, the birds in their amber, the
imminent accident, fire flaring and ghastly,
the explosion's penumbra, in one passed
street, the crumple wave of pressure as two
cars collided, but nothing would answer,
obdurate and fatal, nothing would turn,
adamant as steel, everything was falling
though nothing had fallen: the couple,
sprawling onto their bed in one hushed
apartment; the standing curtain of droplets
in another room's shower. Things want
the conclusions they are given: waiters
shouldering the double kitchen doors,
or that man I was, frozen, half standing,
the wine glass, the pasta, in endless poured
portraits, everything on pause but that one
woman leaving, the only movement, always
and pitiless, her dress, her back, walking away.

Sean O'Brien

The Runners

The elegant women who run with their dogs
through the graveyard, where have they been before now?
They are so self-possessed, yet too preoccupied
with elsewhere and with afterwards to be
entirely present. To be forty-odd and run like that
seems close to immortality. They glide on
through the sunlit pools between the lime-trees,
down to where the tunnelled shade begins
among the older tombs with ironwork
and obelisks and disregarded claims
to time's attention. There they pause
to take a call, or block one. They must have it
all to do, like emissaries
from a new creation, one that like our own
is taken up with its supreme particulars.
I wish that we could be each other's witnesses,
as if I were the past for you, as you for me,
the moment when the cherry-tree
unsleeves its ice-pink trumpery
and turns to dying, while the blackbirds pick
dispassionately among the stones
to pass the time, as though this morning's
not the thing itself, the first hot day,
but instead a late revision of the future
playing out in real time, able to predict
our chances to the second,
only somehow set aside, like good advice
that in the moment of its giving
wears its welcome out. I see you
pause before the tunnel's mouth, your phones
aloft like torches, and I see your dogs,

so loving and so eager for the off,
and now you see them too and smile
and glide away into the dark.

Pádraig Ó Tuama

Liquorice, Mint and Seasalt

I bought the scarf and wrapped it
round my neck. Soft wool,
speckled autumn.
Even I could see it made me
look like me.

When I showed it to you, you
took it from me,
closed your eyes and smelt it, said it
smelt of me already:
liquorice, mint and seasalt.

Eyes still shut you inhaled a little deeper
wrapped it round you,
smiled that smile you smile
inviting me to kiss you.

Sandeep Parmar

from **Faust**

vi.

Kernels of rain   or *seeds* of rain
    is how raindrops translate

so that even the rain is not itself
                when you wait mouth open
                looking sceptical or just pulling
                at the dry earth with broken lips.

Who will plant the rain   in a hearse so that the moon blooms
                                        from his heart?
Grandfather, laid out and burnt like a stoic length of chaff,
his mind a prophecy of smoke.
    Two rupees in his breast pocket and a slip of white, neatly folded,
        with his son's address on it.

Smoke that is not rain nor wheat but leans
into them both like a fever
unmatched by the living.

There   he says, in a blue of white,
that is all you ever needed to know about wheat.

vii.

The wheat came apart in her hands

her hands came apart in the grass

her body a field

the field her body

innumerable hands would bury

Carry the charge

the imprisoned lightning
of her name

Rhiya Pau

Salutation

Inhale
the morning.
He drags lead legs
from beneath the covers.
Squinting, he greets the sun,
fingers together
and the heels of his hands,
palms almost touching.
Exhale,
wooden arms
dispel as he reaches
skyward.
Balanced on his toes,
the puppeteer pulls
at the thread of his spine.
Inhale
his head to his knees.
He bows, folds, creaks.
The tips of his fingertips
scrape carpet.
Behind him,
his right knee bends.
Exhale
rich relief.
The sun on his back
extends his leg back,
arches his back.
Inhale

Exhale
    cloudy cataract,
      arterial pressure,
        a swelling of the feet,
        a shedding of the skin.
    A body to worship.
All hail
   body of memory,
   balancing act,
the strength of the spine,
   resilient lifeline
that he places piece by piece,
   on the school yard.
Heads up, he is a cobra,
   quiet and controlled,
     and fluid of form,
       loose,
     and pliant,
     and charming.   *Exhale*

Michael Pedersen

We Are Other People to Other People

Fifteen years after first asking
I still wobble on whether my dad
gets lonely at golf, the long weight
of a duffed drive, the lost ball's
penalty point. That dog of his
killed by a car, unmourned
for fear of the slagging.
A reprinted requiem of photos
of Dad in the scratty breeks
umpteen sizes over, belted
by rope. Is dirt-poor & Danish
really a master caveat, a bung so as
we might continue to issue emotion
like a weather forecast?

Our language moving with us—
through & past us. The fickle currency
of rain: not for hiding from
but hiding in; capable
of stream & harvest whilst sticking
to puddle & pot-plant. Dad,
have I ever really asked you?
Don't go before I do,
before I come fish-belly-up
wings clipped & straight to it.
We snorkel before we scuba
because a beginning is a limit—
not a deep dive we'd both get lost in,
just a lungful. Just a gasp.

Geoffrey Philp

Virtual Thanksgiving

Inside a local supermarket, open for last-
minute shoppers – nurses, cashiers, waiters,
front line workers who can't afford a day off –
I lost track of time as I hurried through aisles
laden with sweet potato pies and candied yams,
in search of painkillers to relieve my migraines
that have flared since the virus crept into our lives,
and glimpsed a cornucopia, like the one I'd seen
with my mother on our first Thanksgiving
when I confessed I couldn't enjoy a holiday
that celebrated colonisers, who repaid
Wampanoag hospitality by beheading
the Massasoit's son, or how undercover
agents had spurred sufferers, who had borne
the insults of empire, to unleash anarchy
on our streets, murder on our beaches.

As she stared at the horn filled with plums,
pears and pomegranates spilling over the rim,
tears rolled down my mother's cheeks
when she remembered the empty shelves
she'd left the year before when she promised
to send for my sister and me.

Yet she listened patiently and said, 'I hope
you won't become a man who measures his life
by hard times, by sorrows that hide in our closets,
lingering in the corners of our rooms, for grief
can twist you into someone you barely recognise
in the mirror before you plunge into traffic
and the busyness of paperwork and bills.
I am grateful that my mother left the bustle
of Montego Bay to live in Westmoreland

with my father, who sold his last cow
so I could attend teachers' college
in Kingston and that today – even if it's only
the three of us – we can share a meal.'

While I waited in the checkout lane
with other masked customers, my phone
buzzed with a text from my wife – I was late
for the family meeting. My headache could wait.
I left the bottle on the counter and headed home
to raise my glass with my sister in Orlando,
my children in Georgia and Miami, cousins
in Colombia, each on a private screen.
For though we'd celebrate a virtual Thanksgiving
in this year when so many chairs
are missing at our tables, it is sufficient grace.

Stav Poleg

The Letter

Think of it as an installation –
on a glass table, a ceramic-blue
plate – an invitation –

margarita on ice, a hand reaching
for an orange segment, perhaps
it is summer, the changing

of weather. Perhaps you've just
got off the train. The sky like a boy playing
with sunset – you don't know

how it happened, you don't have to
explain. The street is a sunflower
field. The sea, an ongoing

question. Some things
are like this – the traffic, the trees –
an aesthetic dispute – an oscillation –

and far off – the forest
of uneven streets – a karaoke bar
pulsing heat and new

weather. How the light
takes hold of the traffic, the river's dark
floor. How the dark travels

upwards – the coal-silver stars
like a far-off vacation, the inconsistency
of a moon crescent – you know

how it works – it's midsummer, the distance
of stars moving further, the rain
coming in

like a fine stage-direction. Think of it
as a study in pain against
language – the river, the trees –

there's always a thought moving
closer, an unscheduled thunder, a storm
in a picture you're still holding

close. I have to admit – I didn't expect
to see you this early, carrying
a letter – the same one

you tore into pieces years and countries
ago. I think what happened
is this –

you must have managed
to go back in time. Time? Think of it
as a provocation –

a yellow leaf caught in blue-bicycle
weather, a train testing distance
with an inaccurate

question, an equation of words against
speed. It's been raining all day but look –
you have managed to draw your way

here. There are so many windows
in the towering building over the bridge
but only one window

is lit with waves of blue and dark
green. Think of it as a repetition –
on the seventh floor

a woman is watching the same film
she's never able to watch. Some things
are too close, and how often

they move even closer
in films. But this evening, as the rain
plays with darkness across the landscape

of streets, she's leaning against
the half-open window, running a thought
at full speed. The moon –

a recurring wrong
question. The street, a loose
string. Perhaps you've been running for days

in this weather. Perhaps you've just
got off the train. And yes,
there was never

a letter, only a chamber – the movement
of words against words. You don't have
to explain. Some letters

open and close
like an unwritten rumour
but they matter, they matter. How else

would you walk in this wide field
of thought – the moon as a hot-air balloon,
the night – a train

station. You don't know
how it happens. You don't know
how it happens.

Jacob Polley

Little Things

The days are long, the borage flowers blue
and our back yard vibrating now with bees
and hoverflies. We know there should be more.
Memory's sunlight swarms with little things
and remembered moonlit darkness, too,
when even from inside we'd hear their wings
beating like eyelashes. So many eyes
beating at both sides of the glass, the air
alive and us back then. Our memories:
what use are they? The getting in our hair,
our mouths, the flutter-tickle on our skins.
The world is what you touch, what touches you.
They visited, alighting on our bodies,
and we thought hardly anything was there.

Shivanee Ramlochan

Canefield

The girl that rises from the canefield will have blood on her thighs.
Don't run from her ghost.
Stop. Stand there, in the tall sugar.
Let her taste your sweat. Let her lick the litany
of your children's names from your diamond-cut bera.

Her name is Kaloutie. Fit, bony-knees like sharp moth wings,
Drowned in the village well her first year on this island, heavy
Pregnant and thirteen.

Her name is Indrawatti. Heavy voice of hot ghee honeying each
    bhajan,
Hair scraped back from her forehead with the flat of her hand
    anointed in coconut oil,
Holy mandir woman of ragged nails who died of field work, house
    work, bed work.
Collapsed, facedown in the ghee vat, at thirty.

Her name, too, is secret.
Her name is her father picking up a cutlass and telling her to run.
Her name is the bareness of her feet on the rain-drunk brown
    earth,
a splattering of terrors slicking from the pitch pine floorboard to
    the unpaved yard,
and her name is in the pulse of the dholak, her name is what she
    hears from the puja down the dirt road
while fleeing from that killing, and though she has been dead
    before the end of indenture,
if you find yourself in the canefields past midnight she may give
    you her name, her secret name.
She may tell you how she was killed. She may show you the site
    where she was held down.
And it is your job not to look away. And it is your job to listen.

Yvonne Reddick

In Oils

1

I was nine, when my father made me leave –
he drilled an emirate with straight-ruled borders.
The heat on the runway like the breath of a foundry.
My Narnia books arrived after their voyage
along the Suez Canal, in the sea-freight.
Wearing shorts was forbidden – even for men.

Mirage city, under the warp-shimmer of fifty degrees.
Sun-beaten metal. Lightstruck glass,
the bombed-out bridge to Bubiyan Island.
At the sandstone hill on the edge of Iraq,
herdsmen turned camels loose to trigger landmines.

At school, they preached that oil was fossil light:
one barrelful did twelve years' human work.
Dad's friends talked Bonny Light, Brent Blend,
Sour Heavy Crude, counting days in gallons.
Oil was refined, but its temper had a flashpoint –

2

Fragments of Kuwait resurface. Shots, voices on the TV,
half-remembered images, hushed discussions after my light
was turned out.

NAYIRAH
Only ash and rubble was left.
My sister with my five-day old nephew travelled across the desert.
No milk for the baby.

KUWAITI STUDENT
My head was bleeding. I crawled over to Samir,
trying to revive him.
I thought he had been pretending, like me.
Then I saw the bullet hole in his head.

ARCHIVAL FOOTAGE
Wellheads, fire-trenches, the sea alight. Planes and satellites
watching smoke-trails.

CANADIAN FIREFIGHTER
Midday, but when you could see the sky,
it didn't last.
I told them, there's no words
to describe what you're fixed to go into.

KUWAITI OIL ENGINEER
The burning oil-well howled –
sounded like a plane engine.
The Canadians capped the pipes,
then we put in new blowout preventers.
Six billion barrels of light, sweet crude.

ARCHIVAL FOOTAGE
Birds wading in the slick-ponds, a hoopoe drinking petroleum.
The oiled eagle panting for water.

IRAQI REPORTER
They used to call this the City of Peace.
(The first bombs fell at two-thirty.)
Baghdad was a ghost town in the morning,
no electricity or running water.

ARCHIVAL STILLS
Airstrike on the Basra road – the man clawed at the windscreen,
trying to smash free before the petrol tank blew. The camera
blinked at his burnt-out sockets.

It's seared into my memory, he was fighting
to save his life till he was completely burned up.

3

Between fjords and the Firth, the rig whirred
from its crown-block to the pit of its stress-cage –
my father left at dawn to work the offshore fields.
He grafted with roughnecks and a crude-talking toolpusher:
their toil slaked fuel lines, lit flarestacks, stoked motors.
Farther north, the trickle and tick of ice floes.
That year's gales uprooted dunes, hurled gulls
along Union Street; the derrick braced its anchors,
strained against the storm-surge.
                                    His chair sat empty.
The desk paperweight: a drop of Brent crude
globed in glass, the tarry slick levelling when I tilted it.
I tried to pray for breezes to ferry him home,
but all I could invoke were fields of North Sea oil:
Magnus, Beatrice, Loyal.

4

From Anchorage, Calgary, Houston or Galveston
Dad returned, jet-lagged and running fumes,
to plant English lavender on Texan time.
I'd see him at the sink, scrubbing his hands:
'I've fixed the engine!' He'd show his palms –
I watched him scouring skin that wouldn't come clean.
His shirts would smell of earth and gasoline.

* * *

He set off to go hiking, as he had a hundred and sixty-
six times before (he made a note of every hill). But when
night came, Dad still had not returned. The ridge of

the Grey Corries: Hill of the Fawn's Valley, the Castle, Peak of the Brawling Corrie.

We rang the police, who rang Mountain Rescue. They didn't set off until the following morning. (Walkers often get lost and show up in time for breakfast.)

It was his car that they spotted first, without him in it. Then his backpack, just upstream of the waterfall.

John from Mountain Rescue wept soundlessly as he drove us to the pool near the rapids. They found Dad lying face down. The rocks had torn his face.

Cold shock, a fall, the heart. No one knows exactly what happened. And I can't write any more. Don't ask me to write more.

Deryn Rees-Jones

Consider the Lilies

In the last days we had agreed.
O, there would be tenderness.

Wildfires in the park, the ice
breaking and the songy whine
of breakage.

How I wanted then
to lie face down in the white sheets
and slip out from my body.

In a photo — y bryfedog — the Snowdon lily
tucked in the grey rock of the mountain.
Her green, fronding reach.
The force of starry openness.

Poems leant forwards, leant back
into the strain of things. I wept
like a caricature. I removed all question marks
from my devices.

You could wait years to see her bloom.

And all I wanted, then, was for her — bright flower —
to be nothing
but herself and there
as we lifted our selves up to the world
with burning beautiful faces.

With thanks to Bernadette McBride

Dean Rhetoric

How to Unlearn Yourself Completely

I am mostly not made of hands,

or whatever thoughts lean on
to numb before masturbation,

or the parts of a body
I have never learned to use,

that shake under the constant weight
of some imagined destination,

of fist prints inside that just won't straighten
no matter how many times

I   punch   punch   punch   them out

I didn't mean to laugh,
slack-jawed at the punctured air,

or the cracked glass between each sleeve
of its gradually bruising light.

Please understand,
if you suffocate these things for long enough,

nothing really hurts.

Roger Robinson

Nineties Soul Soundtracks Make Everywhere into Somewhere

Even stopping at the gas station is better when you're listening to Keith Sweat singing 'Make It Last Forever'. Johny is running the music for this hour-and-a-bit-long trip. We head out on the motorway to the sounds of D'Angelo's iconic Rhodes piano introducing 'Brown Sugar', and by now we are both singing the lyrics, and then *boom* Erykah Badu's 'Appletree' kicks in and the sky is full of grey, bruised cloud and the leaves of the trees look a deep moss-green and the vibe continues song after song. We talk a bit about European soul; I talk about Omar and Johny introduces me to Stephen Simmonds. The lane markings are passing us at speed, the trees look in through the windshield at us singing Jodeci's 'If You Believe in Love' at the top of our voices. Until the trees open out into the stone-grey buildings of Edinburgh with Zap Mama's 'Bandy Bandy' and we're there.

Declan Ryan

Ethiopia Shall Stretch Forth Her Hands

Joe Louis, mid-clinch,
is lifting his opponent –
the six-foot-six 'Ambling Alp', Primo Carnera –
into the air.
In the Hague,
Italian and Ethiopian officials
have come to the end of their first day
of arbitration talks.
Here, in the Yankee Stadium,
Carnera will sink to his knees
'slowly, like a great chimney that had been dynamited'.

For breakfast this morning, Carnera consumed
a quart of orange juice, two quarts of milk,
nineteen pieces of toast, fourteen eggs,
a loaf of bread and half a pound of Virginia ham.
If he took the *Washington Post*
he would have seen a cartoon showing himself and Louis in the ring.
The illustrated Louis cast a dreadlocked shadow,
his shadow wore a crown.

Louis starts throwing bombs in the sixth round
and knocks the Italian down twice
before a right-left combination
ends the fight.
Louis will touch a glove to Carnera's lower back
after the bell, and return to his corner
without celebration.

Louis has been given seven commandments
by his new manager to ensure he progresses
towards a title shot unhampered
by comparisons to Jack Johnson.

He is never to have his picture taken with a white woman.
He is never to go to a nightclub alone.
There will be no soft fights.
There will be no fixed fights.
He will never gloat over a fallen opponent.
He will keep a 'dead pan' in front of the cameras.
He will live and fight clean.

In 1964, Martin Luther King, Jr will write,
'More than twenty-five years ago, one of the southern states
adopted a new method of capital punishment.
Poison gas supplanted the gallows.
In its earliest stages, a microphone was placed inside
the sealed death chamber so that scientific observers
might hear the words of the dying prisoner.
The first victim was a young Negro.
As the pellet dropped into the container,
and the gas curled upward,
through the microphone came these words:
"Save me, Joe Louis. Save me, Joe Louis. Save me, Joe Louis . . ."'

Jacqueline Saphra

Yom Kippur

By afternoon I am hallucinating
salted caramel which is good for poetry
because nobody wants implacably sweet
in this age of irony and now they tell us salt
won't clog our hearts after all so maybe
it's okay that today, as the godless
cycle in secular joy round the car-free streets
of Jerusalem and hungry Jews everywhere
grow increasingly bad-tempered, I still
hold these grudges; lovely stodgy lumps
at the bottom of my empty atheist stomach
although I no longer remember why
and cannot therefore advise my son
to prostrate himself before Justin Bieber
for insulting him repeatedly on twitter,
or my daughter to sweetly forgive
those girls for guessing her password
and reading her text messages especially
considering my own sins are so old
and wide and manifold and even as the salt
is drying on my lashes I cannot bring myself
to say sorry to my own dead mother whom
I should have venerated, but once told
to fuck off out of my life, or to a lost friend
who, even now, I dare not name, upon whom
I may or may not have once inflicted
terrible wrongs I cannot even now recall
or to the children drowned near the shore
to whom I give scant portions my morning
in momentary horror or for the promises
I may or may not have made to polar bears
and nameless multitudes and I must atone
for the sins of my people

whoever my people are even though
I must atone
goddamit
as if it makes a difference
for my trespasses, omissions, misdemeanours
I must return to the home of my soul
wherever that is
the home I cannot find
however hard I pray

Celia A Sorhaindo

Fragments of Epic Memory

For and after Edward Kamau Brathwaite 11.05.1930—04.02.2020 (RIPE)
and Derek Walcott 23.01.1930—17.03.2017 (RIPE)

Chupes! I see talk continues still about the way we sound:
standard english, pidgin, nation language, dialect, accent,
mellifluous patois. I don't know where the noises I make,
fit, in any of it. No clue which side to take. Dominica born
but Ipswich raised, my husband says on the phone, I sound
so strangely Scottish, and if I try to patois or dialect with this
accent…well…let's just say, it sounding funny funny oui :-).

Yesterday I saw a headline on social media, World's languages
traced back to single African mother tongue. It was a US academic's
'Laughable!!!' comment, that baited me click and read. I also learned
dolphins click communicate their seen images to each other. Today, I'm
reading The Secret History. A machine with metal parts is sliding in
and out. Forming images. An Inca temple…click click click…Pyramids
…the Parthenon, and these words push a piece of magic forward:

a while back I fell. Hit my head hard. Just a hairline crack the
doctor said; no dizzying spells; no black-outs; no noticeable
memory loss; no loss of speech; no need for concern; but for
months after, quiet click click clicks were added to my internal
dialogue. Weird, but not worrying, I thought then. Now, I think,
perhaps history's phenomenal fragments still lie low; beneath
Breath, Eyes, Memory; constantly changing every moment;
affecting each phoneme we make up, sound out, inside or out.

Ahren Warner

from **I'm Totally Killing Your Vibes**

the ageing burgher of Blackpool from whom i have bought a
vintage 28 millimetre lens, says

i'm an AAA++ buyer. and i think, *that's* who i am. i'm an
AAA++ buyer. and i slip and slither

into the bathroom of this once grandiose Ukrainian hotel to
check myself out in the mirror,

and i take off my boxers and socks so i can see the entirety of
my AAA++ buyer's bod,

and i admire the way the scales on my strange reptilian muffintop
glint and glitter in the twenty-five watts

that flickers on, and off, and on to reveal my delicious tail and
my complete lack of nipples

and i extend the rather significant length of my forked tongue,
which is also my nose,

and i lick and sniff the length of this smeared and flaking
Soviet-era mirror,

and i lick and sniff the length of my own reflection, and i
shiver and trill at the taste of iron

and coca and strychnine, which is also the taste of myself,
which is also the taste of money.

After everything, after months of giving me more than I deserved, you have told me it is over. I am sat in the antique German armchair with an inset pegging effect on its teak legs that we paid too much for because of the inset pegging effect on its teak legs, which is considered collectable. I am sat in my studio and the studio manager lets himself in to discuss repairs to the ceiling of my unit to find me sat in an antique German armchair, staring at a property website, tears drizzling my cheeks.

As a child, as a pre-adolescent, I spent all of my pocket money on a birthday present for a pretty girl that did not like me. I remember my father telling me that this was nice, but that a girl needs to like you, and it does not matter what you buy her. I am thinking of this when I ask the studio manager to leave, when I pick up the phone to ring an estate agent, when I view three properties the same afternoon; when after five minutes in the last, most expensive, I take it without bothering to make an offer.

I am convinced that the only way to make things better is to be a better person, to be the person that you will like. I spend months crying in our old bed, fucking Tinder dates in our old bed, hurrying random strangers through rushed avocado-based breakfasts and out of the front door, so I can continue to cry in our old bed.

I am trying to show how much better I am. I am trying to be the functional human that I hope so much you will like again.

the Poet Laureate of the State of Oklahoma does not like my new book.

'this is not how Celan does it,' writes the Poet Laureate of the State of Oklahoma.

and i think: *no shit*...and then i think: how *does* Celan do it?

and then, i think: *hairless, and with the unbleachable stain of living.*

Nerys Williams

Lyrical Invention

Coming from this 'little shit place', as a rugby coach told us in 2018, we learn adaptive strategies. We are mountain people, under the radar, speaking a language that offers protection from direct penetration. Home is broken down, parables of post-industrial, an adventure campground for another country.

Of course, relish the description by A.A. Gill we are 'loquacious, dissemblers, immoral liars, stunted, bigoted, dark, ugly, pugnacious little trolls.' Or, maybe dear reader, if you are into the burn Jeremy Clarkson appeals: 'It's entirely unfair that some people are born fat or ugly or dyslexic or disabled or ginger or small or Welsh. Life, I'm afraid, is tragic.' My friends this tragic life, as we sit in our demesne in soft rainfall. Rod Liddle's 'miserable, seaweed munching, sheep-bothering pinch-faced hill-tribes' comes into mind. Journalists who want our words silenced as 'an appalling and moribund monkey language.' There is a danger in responding too quickly, giving ugly words a permanence, credibility.

Monolingualism is no crime, the curation of other languages is a tricky art, but monoculturalism, the impossibility of fielding doubt into your rhetoric? Doubt makes me wonder if there is a salt mill grinding in the sea. Or, that those mountains are fashioned by a giant god, breathing into life birds, trees and stones. Being didactic creates its own loss, disabling, poor creature with open mouth signing into the world. Leviathans straddling the shapes of their own grammar, splish-splash. Instead, recall how Benjamin Britten's 'This Little Babe' translates into your language. Echo-lalia, how to find narrative accuracy not in the repetition of words, but in timing to music. Caught on quarter inch tape, a reel pack-aged and sent. 'Oh, yes the choral' you nod 'that old stereotype'.

No, what I reference is the force of me, you, us a power of breath
to fall and rise without issuing demands. Being here, colouring a
lyric's final iteration: high notes fading against a cupola, the roof
of a tin shed, the gambrel of a village hall, all the mercury bubbles
unleashed.

Anna Woodford

Go, Mum!

And then, at the end of your life – of our life
together – the walls of the hospital cracked,
the roof fell in. There were doors in ceilings,
in mattresses, in trolleys. Everywhere was an exit.
You were getting away. Sister called and I ran
like I was trapped in a Sharon Olds poem –
and yes, I knew the near body on the side ward spied
out of the side of my eye was you, even as I ran past;
even as the porter gestured back. I knew as you knew
when I burst in through the door as if through the wall
(your superhero). The ward was a rose garden,
a box in a theatre, a shopping centre – anywhere
we had had all our adventures. Heads together,
we bounced on the bed (you were getting higher
and higher). Your hand which would no more
have not squeezed mine than fly, did not squeeze mine.
You were flying, Mum. Bloody Great Death
was at every window, jemmying them open
so you could make clean away in your hospital gown
with your skirt full of scrumped apples – the Dad apple,
the manager apple, the Dr John apple, the Anna apple
polished and balanced on top. Before anyone
could come running with another care plan, another scan,
some Warfarin, you were leaving – your body open-mouthed
at its own agonal breathing. What could I do
but cheer you on – *Go Mum! Go for it! Moira, Go!*

Luke Samuel Yates

Help

There's a man who takes all morning
walking down your road and then
he walks back again with something
round and heavy in a carrier bag.

You'd offer to help him
but you wouldn't want him to feel like he looked
as though he needed help so you don't
but he's still there, passing.

It's snowing the size and shape of cornflakes,
then it stops and the sun comes out
as if after a play to say
So, what did you think?

It's a funny time, your dad tells you,
he doesn't mean that it's April the first,
he doesn't mean that it's 2am
on the last Sunday of October.

Biographies of the shortlisted writers

Jason Allen-Paisant began writing poetry at university. 'As a boy growing up in a single parent household in rural Jamaica, and the first in my family to have done A Levels, let alone go to university, I had never dreamed that one day I would find myself at Oxford,' he says. 'Poetry was a way of reckoning with where I was from, which inevitably meant reckoning with colonialism.'

Self-Portrait as Othello, his second collection, continues and expands this reckoning through the figure of Othello and its valences both Shakespearean and contemporary. The Othello is communed with as much as created, as in the last lines of the collection's first poem: 'I conjure you / furiously'.

Allen-Paisant's debut collection, *Thinking with Trees* (2021), won the OCM Bocas Prize for poetry. He works as a Senior Lecturer in critical theory and creative writing at the University of Manchester.

Kathryn Bevis started writing poems in 2018, after decades of reading, studying and teaching poetry. 'That year, I landed a summer job teaching creative writing to young people,' she writes. 'Beginning to write poems with my students made me realise I had things I wanted to say and that poetry could help me to say them.' Competition success and magazine publication followed, and a full collection is forthcoming with Seren in 2024. Her debut pamphlet, *Flamingo*, came out in 2022.

'My body tells me that she's filing for divorce' was the first poem Bevis wrote after her diagnosis of stage four/metastatic breast cancer. 'The poem arrived very quickly, almost fully formed, which is rare for me,' she notes.

Malika Booker is the co-founder (with Roger Robinson) of the writers' collective 'Malika's Kitchen'. Her first collection, *Pepper Seed*, was shortlisted for the Seamus Heaney Centre Poetry Prize; she is a Teaching Fellow in creative writing at the University of Leeds.

Her shortlisted poem, 'Libation', responds to Kevin Young's poem 'Dreams the Day After Easter' and explores the Caribbean tradition of Nine Night wakes (a subject Booker also drew on for 'Nine Nights', shortlisted for the Forward Prize for Best Single Poem in 2017).

'Libation' also explores the mechanism by which ritual is passed on: 'You there / schooling these youth men in how to be ancestors / in the afterlife.'

Kizziah Burton was born in Jackson, Mississippi, and has spent much of her professional life working in the motion picture industry in Los Angeles. She is currently working on her first collection.

Her shortlisted poem, 'Oh Do You Know The Flower Man', explores coercive control and toxic relationships through the myth of Persephone's abduction by Hades – the 'flower man' of the title. 'The first draft of the poem was overrun with flowers,' Burton writes. 'Like a real garden, the flowers needed to be managed with fences or boundaries, limitations. Once I found the structure, the poem found its container.'

Mary Jean Chan's shortlisted collection, *Bright Fear*, began in lock-down. Its central sequence, 'Ars Poetica', meditates on poetry in a time of crisis; other poems explore the outbreaks of anti-Asian racism which accompanied the pandemic.

Chan began writing poetry in their freshman year at business school in Hong Kong. 'When I was supposed to be doing finance and accounting problem sets, I found myself looking up novels and poetry anthologies in the university library, where I began jotting down poems whenever I had a quiet moment to myself,' they write. This apprenticeship would bear fruit in their 2019 debut, *Flèche*, which won the Costa Poetry Prize.

Jane Clarke began writing poetry in her mid-40s, but since childhood it had been part of the soundtrack of her life. 'My father quoted lines from Shakespeare, Yeats, Longfellow and the Book of Psalms as he went about his farm work,' she remembers. 'My mother gave me *The Book of A Thousand Poems* when I was five and taught me to recite "The Owl and the Pussy-Cat".'

The six sequences of *A Change in the Air* are rooted in County Roscommon and County Wicklow, and range across subjects from a mother's dementia diagnosis to the area's mining heritage to a family's experience of the First World War. Clarke's advice for poets starting out is to pay attention to when 'a memory, an image or an emotion catches us like a briar snags a jersey – follow the snag.'

Susannah Dickey's debut collection *ISDAL* arose out of earlier attempts to write about the Isdal Woman, an unidentified woman discovered dead in Norway in 1970. 'About a year, and many bad poems, later, I realised this was a failed endeavour,' writes Dickey. 'The poems were bad and the thinking that was going into writing them was increasingly making me uncomfortable. Frustrated, I asked myself why it was that I even wanted to write about the Isdal Woman, why I was so fixated with her, with consuming material about her, and it was from that question that the book emerged. The book is one long attempt to explore that question.'

Dickey is the author of two novels and four pamphlets, most recently *Oh!*. Her advice for anyone starting out writing poetry today is to 'seek Susannah Dickey out at the earliest opportunity and give her a £20 Pizza Hut voucher.'

Zena Edwards has been performing poetry for more than 20 years at venues across London and beyond. Her innovative solo shows – *Security*, *Travelling Light* and *The Fury Project* – combine poetry and theatre; André Naffis-Sahely has described her as 'more an orchestral conductor than a solo performer'.

Edwards is currently working towards her first collection. 'It's a story of embodiment of the ancestral line,' she writes. 'It will touch on themes of the body and personal sovereignty, belonging and home, spirituality and faith, nature and environmental awareness.'

Nidhi Zak/Aria Eipe's shortlisted poem, 'And our eyes are on Europe', was commissioned by Poetry Ireland, the Museum of Literature Ireland, ANU and Landmark Productions as part of a year-long project to celebrate the centenary of the publication of James Joyce's *Ulysses*. The poem incorporates phrasing from the novel's 'Cyclops' episode, in which 'Joyce considers questions of citizenship, belonging, identity and cosmopolitanism still relevant today.' Eipe hopes 'that the poem's echoes might invoke the possibility of responding to acts of inhospitality with advances of love.'

Eipe's debut collection, *Auguries of a Minor God*, was published by Faber in 2021 and described by Seán Hewitt as 'heralding the arrival of an assured and compassionate new voice'.

Rowan Evans is a composer and sound artist as well as a poet; field recording, with its possibilities of translation from the non-human, is central to his work. The poems in *A Method, A Path* play with these and other forms of translation, especially from Old English (Evans' PhD thesis examined late Modernist responses to early Medieval texts). His pamphlet from Guillemot Press, *The Last Verses of Beccán*, won the 2019 Michael Marks Award.

'Working within the experimental tradition, it's encouraging to see the lyric ambiguity and formal play I've learned from older writers recognised in this way,' Evans writes. 'I'm glad that new audiences will continue to arrive at the book, and might turn to hear its spooked and many-headed call.'

Kit Fan grew up in Hong Kong before moving to the UK aged 21; reviewing *The Ink Cloud Reader* in the *Guardian*, Rebecca Tamás described the 'complicated mixture of love, danger and anguish that infuses the writer's relationship with the city of his birth.' He has two previous collections: *Paper Scissors Stone* and *As Slow as Possible*.

'I've always been sceptical of the first person in poetry,' writes Fan. 'Even though I've used it countless times, I often feel it is *it*, the all-allusive *I*, who consumes and uses me.' Formally innovative (every poem in *The Ink Cloud Reader* has a different, mostly invented form), Fan's poems refract that 'all-allusive *I*' into something new and multivocal. Imagining the Chinese calligrapher Wang Xizhi washing his brush, Fan wonders, 'Would he have seen himself / in the ink-surface that had turned into / a mirror?'

Safiya Kamaria Kinshasa's poetry arises out of dance and choreography – she describes herself as a 'choreopoet'. *Cane, Corn & Gully* uses labanotation (a method of scoring dance) to recreate the dances of Black Barbadian women across history. 'I wrote when I felt expansive, so every poem is tethered to a sense of triumph,' Kinshasa writes. 'The Black Barbadian women win in my collection; in the history books we are trauma victims, flesh and maybe some bone (rarely a backbone), but in *Cane, Corn & Gully* we are so special.'

Kinshasa began writing poetry seriously after an encounter with Jacob Sam-La Rose at the 2018 Forward Prize ceremony. He gave her three writing challenges; a few months later Kinshasa writes, 'we met at a poetry event, he asked me how I was doing, and I informed him I didn't just complete his challenges, but I worked on my poetry and read every single day, and I had a new notebook full of poems, ideas and most importantly questions.'

Momtaza Mehri was the 2018 Young People's Laureate for London. *Bad Diaspora Poems* found its shape over the subsequent five years; describing the book's gestation, she writes that, for her, 'the writing process begins with theoretical tussling. I think through an obsession or a wound for a while, talking it out with others, opening myself up to how it reveals itself anew in my life. I stay sensitised.'

Her advice for new poets starting out is simple: 'Seek out the nooks poets hide in. Have a healthy scepticism of genres and groupings. Go where the terror is.'

Michael Pedersen started out writing poetry in Scots for his school magazine. 'The beautiful quirks of the language offered up masks and obfuscations to keep the emotional beat of what I was writing hidden away from prying eyes,' he writes. But 'it was the discovery that poems could be profane and political, as well as supremely soppy and sincere, that really got me hooked – I guess it's akin to kittens having sharp claws.'

Pedersen is the co-founder of Neu! Reekie!, a literary production house organising live shows, festivals and anthologies. He has recently published his second poetry collection, *The Cat Prince & Other Poems*, as well as a memoir, *boy friends*.

Bohdan Piasecki founded Poland's first poetry slam. He currently lives in Birmingham, where he is an Assistant Professor in Creative Writing, having been for many years the Midlands producer for Apples & Snakes.

'We build poems out of bits of language,' Piasecki writes. 'My bits come from three different languages: Polish, my family's language, the one with which I grew up; French, the language of my education (a long story); and English, the language I chose, the one in which I live. In my daily life all of these are mixed up. We like to talk of first languages or mother tongues, but my experience – and, I have been assured, that of many migrants like me, and those who live in societies that use more than one language – is different. The languages aren't separate. They are one set of words, one big bag of bits.'

Roger Robinson won the 2019 TS Eliot Prize for his debut collection, *A Portable Paradise*. *Home Is Not A Place*, from which his shortlisted poem is taken, documents in poems and photographs a road trip with the photographer Johny Pitts in a rented red Mini Cooper, in search of the history and traces of Black Britain. Robinson is also the lead vocalist and songwriter for the band King Midas Sound.

Robinson's favourite poets include Kwame Dawes, Natalie Diaz, Pascale Petit, Li Young Lee, Malika Booker, Terrance Hayes, Airea D Matthews: 'They all have an innovative sense of craft and grace.'

Elisabeth Sennitt Clough found a unique source of inspiration for the titular persona of *my name is abilene* – an internet anagram generator, given her own name, returned 'abilene fluorescent nightclothes', and she challenged herself to write a poem using that as a prompt. Sennitt Clough imagined Abilene as 'a metaphorical representation of female pain when a woman is pushed too far'. 'To a certain degree,' she writes, 'Abilene is such an absurd rendering of the heartbroken woman, that I had to move far away from conventional tropes. Abilene is anything but conventional.'

Sennitt Clough's debut pamphlet, *Glass* (2016), won a Saboteur Award; she has published four subsequent collections. The landscape of eastern England, where she lives, is a constant presence across her work; fittingly, she is the founding editor of the *Fenland Poetry Journal*.

Breda Spaight's shortlisted poem, 'The Curse', explores many of the same themes as her debut collection, *Watching the Hawk* (Arlen House), centred around shockingly vivid glimpses of coming-of-age in rural Ireland. In 'The Curse', the birth of a calf recalls what Spaight describes as 'a moment of innocent cruelty between siblings that originates in misogyny'.

Spaight's favourite poets include Anne Sexton, Sharon Olds, Ellen Bass, Dorianne Laux, Danusha Lameris, Tony Hoagland, Stephen Dunn and Li-Young Lee. 'They invite me to enter their open doors,' she writes. 'I love entering the world of the *I*.'

Kandace Siobhan Walker won the White Review Poets' Prize in 2021 for a portfolio of her work. In a subsequent interview, she described what drew her to poetry as an art form: 'With poetry, I can be clear and inconclusive at the same time. It's more gestures than arguments. I can feel my way around a thought without feeling like I need to come up with an answer.'

Walker began writing poetry while studying creative writing at university, but she found the dynamics and machinations of the publishing world intimidating. Her solution was to decouple her writing from the need for publication: 'working in a bookshop back home, I would read at the till and spend the time I wasn't serving customers writing notes on blank receipt paper. When I felt that I was learning why the poems I admired were able to do what they did, I think then I started to feel like I was a poet.'

Eric Yip grew up in Hong Kong. 'Because English wasn't the language I used with family and friends, writing in it gave me a remoteness that I found freeing,' he writes; the tensions between that freedom and the colonial baggage of the language feed into his shortlisted poem, 'Fricatives'. In the poem's words, 'You must learn to submit / before you can learn. You must be given a voice / before you can speak.'

Yip is currently studying economics at the University of Cambridge. 'If I could talk to myself from two or three years ago, I'd tell him to read adventurously, to be curious and empathetic, and to always have a beginner's heart,' writes Yip. 'Nothing is unimportant.'

Publisher acknowledgements

AJ Akoto · Daughterhood · *Unmothered* · Arachne Press

Jason Allen-Paisant · The Picture and the Frame · Self-Portrait as
  Othello II · *Self-Portrait as Othello* · Carcanet

Anthony Anaxagorou · Float · *Heritage Aesthetics* · Granta

Vicci Bentley · The Policeman's Daughter · Mslexia Women's Poetry
  Competition

Tara Bergin · Penetration · *Savage Tales* · Carcanet

Liz Berry · Eliza · *The Home Child* · Chatto & Windus

Kathryn Bevis · My body tells me that she's filing for divorce · Second
  Light Poetry Competition

Laurie Bolger · Parkland Walk · The Moth Poetry Prize

Malika Booker · Libation · *The Poetry Review*

Kizziah Burton · Oh Do You Know The Flower Man · Mslexia Women's
  Poetry Competition

Mary Jean Chan · Love for the Living · Ars Poetica XIII · *Bright Fear* ·
  Faber

Chen Chen · The School of Australia · *Your Emergency Contact Has
  Experienced an Emergency* · Bloodaxe Books

Jane Clarke · Spalls · At Purteen Harbour · *A Change in the Air* ·
  Bloodaxe Books

Geraldine Clarkson · Leperskin Coat · *Medlars* · Shearsman Books

Rishi Dastidar · *from Pretanic*: The Brexit book of the dead · *Neptune's
  Projects* · Nine Arches Press

Susannah Dickey · Sex sells · Outtake #3 · *ISDAL* · Picador

Zena Edwards · Human: This Embodied Knowledge

Nidhi Zak/Aria Eipe · And our eyes are on Europe · Poetry Ireland

Akwaeke Emezi · Disclosure · *Content Warning: Everything* ·
  Bloomsbury Poetry

Rowan Evans · On Eglond · *A Method, A Path* · Bloomsbury Poetry

Kit Fan · Mother's Ink · Delphi · *Ink Cloud Reader* · Carcanet

Katie Farris · In the Early Days of a Global Pandemic · *Standing in the
  Forest of Being* · Pavilion Poetry, Liverpool University Press

Salena Godden · While Justice Waits · *Wasafiri Magazine*

Em Gray · Symbiosis · Mslexia Women's Poetry Competition

Elle Heedles · Rain Noise · *Rain Noise* · Partus Press

Selima Hill · People in Taxis · *Women in Comfortable Shoes* · Bloodaxe
Books

Emma Jeremy · i talk about the beach · *Sad Thing Angry* · Out-Spoken
Press

Majella Kelly · Forget · *The Speculations of Country People* · Penguin Books

Victoria Kennefick · SUPER KING · *Daily Telegraph Review*

Safiya Kamaria Kinshasa · Gully · Avoid Direct Contact With the Skull ·
Cane, Corn & Gully · Out-Spoken Press

Karl Knights · The Night Before My PiP Tribunal I See My Dead ·
The Dark Horse

Zaffar Kunial · Empty Words · *England's Green* · Faber

Nick Laird · Talking to the Sun in Washington Square · *Up Late* · Faber

Vanessa Lampert · Tower · *Say It With Me* · Seren

Fran Lock · Of Familiars/I Shall Go Into a Hare · *White/Other* ·
the87press

Adam Lowe · Like This (Polari Version) · *Patterflash* · Peepal Tree Press

Arji Manuelpillai · The Expendables · *Improvised Explosive Device* ·
Penned in the Margins

Momtaza Mehri · Fluke by Any Other Name is a Flight Number ·
On Memory as Molasses as Muscle as Miasma · *Bad Diaspora Poems* ·
Jonathan Cape

Joseph Minden · Historiography · *Poppy* · Carcanet

Emma Must · Holloway Letters · *The Ballad of Yellow Wednesday* · Valley
Press

Daljit Nagra · Dramatis Personae · Canto I: Prologue · *Indiom* · Faber

Selina Nwulu · Lips · *A Little Resurrection* · Bloomsbury Poetry

Pádraig Ó Tuama · Liquorice, Mint and Sea Salt · *Feed the Beast* ·
Broken Sleep Books

Damen O'Brien · Scene in Medias Res · Bridport Prize / Redcliffe Press

Sean O'Brien · The Runners · *Embark* · Picador

Sandeep Parmar · Faust vi and vii · *Faust* · Shearsman Books

Rhiya Pau · Salutation · *Routes* · Arachne Press

Michael Pedersen · The Cat Prince · Neu! Reekie!

Michael Pedersen · We Are Other People to Other People · *The Cat
Prince & Other Poems* · Little, Brown Book Group / Corsair

Geoffrey Philp · Virtual Thanksgiving · *Archipelagos* · Peepal Tree Press

Bohdan Piasecki · Almost Certainly · I Am Loud Productions

Winners of the Forward Prizes

Best Collection

2022 · Kim Moore · *All the Men I Never Married* · Seren

2021 · Luke Kennard · *Notes from the Sonnets* · Penned in the Margins

2020 · Caroline Bird · *The Air Year* · Carcanet

2019 · Fiona Benson · *Vertigo & Ghost* · Jonathan Cape

2018 · Danez Smith · *Don't Call Us Dead* · Chatto & Windus

2017 · Sinéad Morrissey · *On Balance* · Carcanet

2016 · Vahni Capildeo · *Measures of Expatriation* · Carcanet

2015 · Claudia Rankine · *Citizen: An American Lyric* · Penguin Books

2014 · Kei Miller · *The Cartographer Tries to Map a Way to Zion* · Carcanet

2013 · Michael Symmons Roberts · *Drysalter* · Jonathan Cape

2012 · Jorie Graham · *PLACE* · Carcanet

2011 · John Burnside · *Black Cat Bone* · Jonathan Cape

2010 · Seamus Heaney · *Human Chain* · Faber & Faber

2009 · Don Paterson · *Rain* · Faber & Faber

2008 · Mick Imlah · *The Lost Leader* · Faber & Faber

2007 · Sean O'Brien · *The Drowned Book* · Picador

2006 · Robin Robertson · *Swithering* · Picador

2005 · David Harsent · *Legion* · Faber & Faber

2004 · Kathleen Jamie · *The Tree House* · Picador

2003 · Ciaran Carson · *Breaking News* · The Gallery Press

2002 · Peter Porter · *Max is Missing* · Picador

2001 · Sean O'Brien · *Downriver* · Picador

2000 · Michael Donaghy · *Conjure* · Picador

1999 · Jo Shapcott · *My Life Asleep* · OUP

1998 · Ted Hughes · *Birthday Letters* · Faber & Faber

1997 · Jamie McKendrick · *The Marble Fly* · OUP

1996 · John Fuller · *Stones and Fires* · Chatto & Windus

1995 · Sean O'Brien · *Ghost Train* · OUP

1994 · Alan Jenkins · *Harm* · Chatto & Windus

1993 · Carol Ann Duffy · *Mean Time* · Anvil Press

1992 · Thom Gunn · *The Man with Night Sweats* · Faber & Faber

Best First Collection

2022 · Stephanie Sy-Quia · *Amnion* · Granta

2021 · Caleb Femi · *Poor* · Penguin Books

2020 · Will Harris · *Rendang* · Granta

2019 · Stephen Sexton · *If All the World and Love Were Young* · Penguin Books

2018 · Phoebe Power · *Shrines of Upper Austria* · Carcanet

2017 · Ocean Vuong · *Night Sky with Exit Wounds* · Jonathan Cape

2016 · Tiphanie Yanique · *Wife* · Peepal Tree Press

2015 · Mona Arshi · *Small Hands* · Pavilion Poetry, Liverpool University Press

2014 · Liz Berry · *Black Country* · Chatto & Windus

2013 · Emily Berry · *Dear Boy* · Faber & Faber

2012 · Sam Riviere · *81 Austerities* · Faber & Faber

2011 · Rachael Boast · *Sidereal* · Picador

2010 · Hilary Menos · *Berg* · Seren

2009 · Emma Jones · *The Striped World* · Faber & Faber

2008 · Kathryn Simmonds · *Sunday at the Skin Launderette* · Seren

2007 · Daljit Nagra · *Look We Have Coming to Dover!* · Faber & Faber

2006 · Tishani Doshi · *Countries of the Body* · Aark Arts

2005 · Helen Farish · *Intimates* · Jonathan Cape

2004 · Leontia Flynn · *These Days* · Jonathan Cape

2003 · AB Jackson · *Fire Stations* · Anvil Press

2002 · Tom French · *Touching the Bones* · The Gallery Press

2001 · John Stammers · *Panoramic Lounge-Bar* · Picador

2000 · Andrew Waterhouse · *In* · The Rialto

1999 · Nick Drake · *The Man in the White Suit* · Bloodaxe Books

1998 · Paul Farley · *The Boy from the Chemist is Here to See You* · Picador

1997 · Robin Robertson · *A Painted Field* · Picador

1996 · Kate Clanchy · *Slattern* · Chatto & Windus

1995 · Jane Duran · *Breathe Now, Breathe* · Enitharmon

1994 · Kwame Dawes · *Progeny of Air* · Peepal Tree Press

1993 · Don Paterson · *Nil Nil* · Faber & Faber

1992 · Simon Armitage · *Kid* · Faber & Faber

Best Single Poem – Written

2022 · Nick Laird · Up Late · *Granta*

2021 · Nicole Sealey · Pages 22–29, *an excerpt from* The Ferguson Report: An Erasure · *Poetry London*

2020 · Malika Booker · The Little Miracles · *Magma Poetry*

2019 · Parwana Fayyaz · Forty Names · *PN Review*

2018 · Liz Berry · The Republic of Motherhood · *Granta*

2017 · Ian Patterson · The Plenty of Nothing · *PN Review*

2016 · Sasha Dugdale · Joy · *PN Review*

2015 · Claire Harman · The Mighty Hudson · *Times Literary Supplement*

2014 · Stephen Santus · In a Restaurant · Bridport Prize

2013 · Nick MacKinnon · The Metric System · *The Warwick Review*

2012 · Denise Riley · A Part Song · *London Review of Books*

2011 · RF Langley · To a Nightingale · *London Review of Books*

2010 · Julia Copus · An Easy Passage · *Magma*

2009 · Robin Robertson · At Roane Head · *London Review of Books*

2008 · Don Paterson · Love Poem for Natalie 'Tusja' Beridze · *The Poetry Review*

2007 · Alice Oswald · Dunt · *Poetry London*

2006 · Sean O'Brien · Fantasia on a Theme of James Wright · *The Poetry Review*

2005 · Paul Farley · Liverpool Disappears for a Billionth of a Second · *The North*

2004 · Daljit Nagra · Look We Have Coming to Dover! · *The Poetry Review*

2003 · Robert Minhinnick · The Fox in the Museum of Wales · *Poetry London*

2002 · Medbh McGuckian · She Is in the Past, She Has This Grace · *The Shop*

2001 · Ian Duhig · The Lammas Hireling · National Poetry Competition

2000 · Tessa Biddington · The Death of Descartes · Bridport Prize

1999 · Robert Minhinnick · Twenty-five Laments for Iraq · *PN Review*

1998 · Sheenagh Pugh · Envying Owen Beattie · *New Welsh Review*

1997 · Lavinia Greenlaw · A World Where News Travelled Slowly · *Times Literary Supplement*

1996 · Kathleen Jamie · The Graduates · *Times Literary Supplement*

1995 · Jenny Joseph · In Honour of Love · *The Rialto*

1994 · Iain Crichton Smith · Autumn · *PN Review*

1993 · Vicki Feaver · Judith · *Independent on Sunday*

1992 · Jackie Kay · Black Bottom · Bloodaxe Books

Supporting poetry with Forward

In buying this book you have helped Forward support new talent, engage young people and build poetry's audience. Thank you!

The Forward Prizes are the most influential awards for new poetry published in the UK and Ireland, and since 1992 have lauded some of the most recognised names in poetry alongside the most exciting emerging voices. Our books include *Poems of the Decade*, now on the A-Level syllabus. Each October National Poetry Day generates an explosion of activity in communities nationwide, with thousands of amazing events all proving poetry's power to bring people together. In all, our work reaches around 1.2 million people each year.

We are ambitious for poetry's future and work in partnership with publishing, arts, education and community organisations to have the biggest impact. We want to enable more poets, potential poets and poetry lovers to create an art form that is relevant and representative of the UK today.

To find out more about how you can support us and get involved in our work, please email lucy@forwardartsfoundation.org or get in touch on Facebook or Twitter @ForwardPrizes

Feedback

Please scan the QR code to access a short survey. Your views are so important to us – they help us improve our programme and let our funders know how we are doing.